Secret Harvests

Also by

David Mas Masumoto

Silent Strength

Country Voices

Epitaph for a Peach

Harvest Son

Four Seasons in Five Senses

Letters to the Valley

Heirlooms

Wisdom of the Last Farmer

The Perfect Peach
(with Marcy Masumoto and Nikiko Masumoto)

Sense of Yosemite

Changing Season
(with Nikiko Masumoto)

Secret Harvests

A Hidden Story of Separation and
the Resilience of a Family Farm

David Mas Masumoto

ARTWORK BY

Patricia Wakida

 Red Hen Press | *Pasadena, CA*

Book Layout by Mark E. Cull

Library of Congress Cataloging-in-Publication Data

Names: Masumoto, David Mas, author.
Title: Secret harvests: a hidden story of separation and the resilience of
  a family farm / David Mas Masumoto.
Other titles: Hidden story of separation and the resilience of a family
  farm
Description: First edition. | Pasadena, CA: Red Hen Press, [2023]
Identifiers: LCCN 2022016771 (print) | LCCN 2022016772 (ebook) | ISBN
  9781636280776 (hardcover) | ISBN 9781636281032 (trade paperback) | ISBN
  9781636280783 (ebook)
Subjects: LCSH: Masumoto, David Mas—Family. | Japanese American
  farmers—California—Fresno—Biography. | Japanese
  Americans—California—Fresno—Biography. | Japanese
  Americans—California—Fresno—Social conditions—20th century. |
  Sugimoto, Shizuko, 1919-2013. | Disabled
  women—California—Fresno—Biography. | Meningitis—Patients—Biography.
  | Farmers—California—Fresno—Biography. | Fresno (Calif.)—Biography.
Classification: LCC F869.F8 M37 2023 (print) | LCC F869.F8 (ebook) | DDC
  979.4004/9560922—dc23/eng/20220427
LC record available at https://lccn.loc.gov/2022016771
LC ebook record available at https://lccn.loc.gov/2022016772

Publication of this book has been made possible in part through the generous financial support
of Ann Beman.

The National Endowment for the Arts, the Los Angeles County Arts Commission, the Ahmanson
Foundation, the Dwight Stuart Youth Fund, the Max Factor Family Foundation, the Pasadena
Tournament of Roses Foundation, the Pasadena Arts & Culture Commission and the City of Pasa-
dena Cultural Affairs Division, the City of Los Angeles Department of Cultural Affairs, the Audrey
& Sydney Irmas Charitable Foundation, the Meta & George Rosenberg Foundation, the Albert and
Elaine Borchard Foundation, the Adams Family Foundation, Amazon Literary Partnership, the
Sam Francis Foundation, and the Mara W. Breech Foundation partially support Red Hen Press.

First Edition
Published by Red Hen Press
www.redhen.org

For my Aunt Shizuko,
the Sugimoto Family,
and the Masumoto Family—
for their resilience.
—David Mas Masumoto

To my Bachan Miyeko Okamura Kebo
and my Grandma Rose Wada Wakida
—Patricia Wakida

Contents

A family separated by racism
against Japanese Americans and
the discrimination of people with developmental disabilities—
reunited seventy years later,
returning to their roots on a farm
and bound by family secrets.

Every Family Has Secrets

I Farm with Ghosts

I farm with ghosts. They live in our fields. Each peach tree has pruning scars from the generations who worked these orchards. Every vine has been shaped by the hands of workers who returned each year to add their touch to the sculpture. People and their families have etched their marks on my farm, and I, too, hope to leave behind a simple signature on this seemingly ordinary landscape.

Ghosts inhabit our family history; their collective voices contribute to a perspective that shaped my upbringing. They pass on lessons I struggle to understand, sometimes rejecting, other times surrendering to their value, but never ignoring them because they haunt my memories: a worn shovel, a bent peach limb, the twisted trunk of an old grapevine, a family photo, a Buddhist altar—all trigger a rush of stories that can overwhelm.

Memory and reflections fill this book as I learn more about my family's past. We were immigrants from rural Japan, Kumamoto on my father's side and Hiroshima on my mother's side. We were destined to become farmers like generations before us, scratching out a living while carving a niche in the earth. We were Buddhist in a Christian land, settling in the isolated countryside outside of Fresno, California. We were farmworkers, then later farmers of organic peaches, nectarines, apricots, and grapes for raisins. Because of our legacy as immigrants and the incarceration my family endured during World War II, we lacked collections of artifacts. I inherited only a few haunting sketches. Often reserved, we were not a family of storytellers. A silence hovered over family gatherings as I learned to accept and explore the unspoken.

Memories can and should change. Our own stories are fluid, reimagined with new information, corrected with facts, yet anchored in a past as we try to honestly recall and yearn to remember. Documenting these stories forces me to ask: What is the truth and why does it matter? And most importantly, how deeply does one explore dark family issues yet respect distances with a historical tenderness?

One of the ghosts who inhabit our farm is Shizuko, an aunt with an intellectual disability whom we only recently reconnected with. Like a grapevine's wandering canes and tendrils that twist and curl, searching for attachment and support yet reaching for sunlight to strengthen and extend their growth, her story unfolds as an evolving tale buried in the history of immigrants, the saga of racism and discrimination, the deplorable treatment of people with disabilities, and the shroud of family hidden stories, all the while working the earth and trying to plant and extend our roots in American soil.

I am not speaking for Shizuko. I do not speak on behalf of disabled people. Too often many have assumed they know what the disabled community knows and thinks. I remain inadequate to write that story; Shizuko has her own voice and her own way of communicating that I am only beginning to grasp. I try to capture the mosaic of her life as told through family stories combined with research, visits, and interviews.

I cannot fully complete her portrait because of the gaps in her life story. Instead, I can only attempt to grasp the significance of the lost years and decades of her survival and thriving resilience. I am haunted by gaps in family memories, nebulous responses and twisted behavior that must be examined within the context of history—not to uncover excuses but rather reveal family baggage we all must carry and learn to live with. Much of her story continues to be found in a world of secrets to be explored.

I carry the weight of troubled memories. Some are stirred by wondering; others are involuntary, stimulated by the feel of the dirt and sweat on our farm or the aroma of a ripening peach. I attempt to organize them into a narrative but accept the impossibility of the task. No one has a monopoly on the truth, the ghosts of one-hundred-year-old grapevines remind me.

Family stories fill gaps in my sense of history, how I was raised and what I am to become. All families carry the weight of secrets: they can both burden and yet define us. We may deny their existence or seek transparency. Most of the time they linger like baggage generations carry, fully aware of their presence—or not. I search for information, insight, and resolution—or not.

The ghosts in this book are serious and quiet, yet alive. They laugh with a twisted humor and lighter moments, even while showing me that I'm asking the wrong questions.

"Just listen," they seem to whisper to me.
"Just listen."

PART ONE

ARRIVAL

I

The Call—I Thought I Knew My Family

February 2012

Shizuko is sick, sick to death with this long agony. She lays still, her ninety-year-old body motionless. Her wheelchair sits empty. A head pokes in, checking. Waiting for her to die? Or do they look because they care? A roommate whines in the next bed, but Shizuko should be the one requesting help. Now a stroke. Senses leave her body. Rest. The sentence complete. Sleep. Alone again, naturally.

Shizuko was assigned to hospice after spending thirteen years in Golden Cross Nursing Home. Before, she was housed at various state-run institutions, the type you'd see in movies with hundreds of forlorn bodies wandering long, dingy white hallways and rows and rows of beds. For decades, she roamed these halls ceaselessly. She outlived all her roommates.

Her family came as immigrants, picked peaches and grapes in the fields of California, found poverty and racism and yet stayed while struggling to build something. Shizuko avoided the Japanese American internment camps of World War II because she was classified as "retarded," a derogatory term unfortunately commonly used in the past. Her life was branded with confusion.

A tiny woman, a little over four feet tall and weighing only seventy pounds, she was in constant motion, always relentlessly moving, seemingly endlessly active. Even when limited to a wheelchair, she could be left alone, content to shuffle throughout the structures, paddling the floor with her brightly colored, tiny, kid's tennis shoes. A life of pain, illness, separation, departure, and return. Like a ghost, perpetually searching for stolen time.

A phone message from the Wildrose Funeral Home. A solicitation call? I dislike and distrust the phone—I farm, work with dirt, orchards and vineyards stretching along the horizon. I talk more to peaches than people because the trees pretend to listen. I find comfort and order in vine rows: their history I understand and accept.

I grew up in a home where phone calls were supposed to be for important exchanges. I can recall my grandmother Masumoto panicking with the sharp *ring, ring, ring* of the phone, yelling in pidgin Japanese, "Te-re-fon! Te-re-fon!" The rattling clamor followed by the brittle vibration that seemed to linger in the air triggered memories and emotions in her, a feeling I seemed to have inherited. Phone calls typically delivered bad news—like the call you get in the middle of the night that elicits a sick feeling that tightens your stomach.

But a bulletin from a funeral home? I'm too young. But the voice then asks for "Carole Sugimoto," my mom with her maiden name.

I return the call, ready to hang up with the first pitch. Instead, they inquire if Carole is related to a "Shizuko."

"Who?"

I pause. I vaguely recall hearing of a mysterious aunt with "a mental problem," as the family described and no one talked about. I was told that she had died in her youth, part of the Great Depression era when life was messy, especially for the poor.

The woman on the phone continues. She is "searching for next of kin and discovered Carole from your father's obituary."

"What? Who?" I think to myself. I'm confused, uneasy about a stranger talking about my family. Her voice makes me feel uncomfortable. I want to hang up.

"Shizuko Sugimoto, your mom's sister, born in 1919." The voice on the phone then adds, "Institutionalized at various facilities."

I had once heard a story about some state mental institution and this forgotten aunt. But that aunt had passed long, long ago. Gone for seventy years. This news is disruptive and disturbing, a departure from my understanding of family. This simply does not make sense: is there a twisted riddle in my family's past and can I trust this call?

"Shizuko is in Fresno, a few miles from your home and peaches and vineyards," the telephone voice continues. "She's alive, barely."

2

Shikata ga nai—It Can't Be Helped

Shizuko in Japanese means "quiet child." Her name foreshadows her life, a history of struggle and silently overcoming challenges and accepting who she is and what she never will be. Always present in my family is another term, "shikata ga nai." A common Japanese saying which means: "it can't be helped" or "nothing can be done." It will be a blessing and curse that will follow Shizuko as this quiet child searches to find her voice.

Why didn't I know about Shizuko? How can my aunt survive decades of institutional care—alone? Why did no one in my generation know about her? The twisted past of my family history haunts me, a puzzle I'm confronted with, a confrontation I can no longer ignore. I once read a story about Rosemary Kennedy, the intellectually disabled sister of John and Robert Kennedy who was hidden for decades, unfortunately a common practice at that time. But when I think of our family, weren't we a family of farmers who cared for the earth and crops. And people?

I recall a Buddhist minister once offered me some sage words: life is not a problem to be solved but a mystery to be lived. Perhaps this is the world now opening to me and yet I feel anxious, filled with suspicion and skepticism, wondering what is normal.

Each year as winter passes, we look forward with optimism but can never escape the past harvests and disappointments—the odd weather that altered a growing peach or the new arrival of a pest like mealy bugs infesting our vineyards. On an organic farm, especially with permanent crops like stone fruit and grapevines, yesterday shapes tomorrow. How we envision that past affects our futures. We are haunted by the pruning scars embedded in the shape of a tree, eternally wondering if a simple act like snipping a young branch or sawing a tree limb is the proper choice, a life filled with doubt and yet striving to believe and trust we made the right decisions. Hardpan rocks are still scattered in the fields reminding me of the poor quality of the soil that I must continue to enhance and fortify with nutrients and life. The changing climate and droughts alter leaf growth and vigor, and I must find ways to adapt and adjust or stop farming. We may be perpetual pioneers working new fields of life as we struggle to fit in, caught between forces of nature and the human-made demands of markets, sales, and making a living. All the while trying to belong.

But Shizuko is an unknown entity from a past I thought I knew. We have no physical memory of her, no old black-and-white photo with her face. I never heard mention of her presence as part of the family. There was no grave marker with her name. Without documentation, I have nothing to forget because there was nothing to remember. It would be as if our orchards and vineyards were never part of our family farm. We would have no ownership because we had no personal history. I could not work this land completely without the voices of ancestors guiding me as I strive to work with nature and not control her. That's why I chose to farm organically.

Are memories of Shizuko consciously suppressed and buried—and that's the mystery to be solved? I naively ask too much, and little may be gained from opening old wounds. Perhaps it's normal for families to withhold stories. Yet Shizuko's life story has much to teach me. I am called to remember, and a memory is born with questions.

I grew up hearing *shikata ga nai* often. When something didn't work or accidently broke, like a tractor or peach limb, the phrase *shikata ga nai* circulated in daily conversations. During summer harvests on the farm, I heard my father and uncles use the phrase when fruit prices dropped and we were making little or no money—at first, they were angry, then realized they were helpless to determine value. Money could not be the only measure of family wealth. My parents and grandparents employed *shikata ga nai* to describe the daily grind and struggle as they labored in the fields of California as farmworkers. Later, they used that term trying to explain and untangle the Japanese American internment and imprisonment during World War II because they looked like the enemy.

Whenever something felt wrong—a rain on our grapes trying to dry into raisins; the insults because we were Buddhists in a Christian country and my high school English teacher proclaimed, "everyone believes in God;" or in elementary school, believing I was the same as the other kids despite being teased because my eyes and face were different—I heard the phrase from my family.

When I partnered with my father on our family farm, I wondered if peach farmers were eternally at the mercy of nature and human nature. Was this an excuse for errors of the past and a sign of weakness and blind acceptance as we searched for safety? Or could this be a necessary rule for passive resignation and survival as outcasts in a new land? My family seemed to tolerate hardships with a whisper, "*shikata ga nai,*" followed by silence.

I grew confused and perplexed. Our family annals lacked a sense of certainty and predictability. I was unsure where I belonged in my own family story and what voices to trust because I never completely understood when and how to use the phrase.

Adopt. Adapt. Accept.
We are called to remember and unremember.
Shikata ga nai. It can't be helped.

3

Footprints of the Past

Shizuko is born on October 13, 1919. She has no idea of their immigrant family history. Her world is simple and poor. For the first five years of her life, she lives a full childhood, surrounded by brother and sisters. They play, they tease, they run, they hide in the fields while their parents work. She is guided by the only life she knows: the open countryside of farms, the crops growing, the weeds and wildlife flourishing, all part of a natural world that surrounds her. The aroma of a ripening peach, the sound of leaves rustling in the breeze, the caramel scent of grapes drying into raisins—they all create vivid memories of a secure place she can call home. She can look up and see an expansive blue sky surrounding her, embracing her. She can walk familiar country paths in a peaceful silence of trust. She knows of no other reality, and this will empower her to survive.

I need to learn more about Shizuko and gather information, yet I hesitate; I had never challenged my mother about family secrets. A part of me stirs with anger, wondering why this person was hidden.

"Everyone believes she had passed away years ago . . ." my mom initially replies.

I pause. Should I share the mysterious phone call from the funeral home and belie my mother's reality? Instead, I grow curious, like a good detective, gathering information, searching for clues, wanting to know more. Our family farm story unfolds, some rich stories with details: the family worked in the fields with their hands, the poverty of immigrants who arrived with nothing and dreamed of something more. Other stories feel specific: I knew that my mother's side of the family came from Hiroshima. She stalls from providing more explanation. I had forgotten that there was an entire set of family she has and will never meet—aunts and uncles left behind, cousins she will never cross paths with. She mentions the atomic bomb and stops, accepting the gaps and the haunting silence of the past.

I grow irritated. How do you know what you don't know? We are taught that history is about facts, as if complete accounts have been properly researched, recorded and passed down. Lapses in memory and incomplete narratives are part of my story too. I wonder what has been forgotten or erased—and unremembered.

My maternal grandparents came from the rural countryside, leaving villages in Hiroshima, carrying hope to foreign places called Fresno, Selma, Fowler, and Del Rey. They embodied an immigrant's story. Pushed from the old country by dark forces beyond their control—poverty, power, politics, and fear. Across an ocean lies a new land pulling them into the light of dreams. A wave in immigrants, part of a Japanese diaspora that included America, Brazil, and Peru. They, like many Asians, left a nation that valued a sense of group identity, a collective whole, and journeyed to a land dominated by capitalism, competition, and individualism. An illusion of belonging shimmered on the horizon. Then the Immigration Act of 1924 limited the number of immigrants allowed entry into the United States and completely excluded all immigrants from Asia, slamming shut the door for other Asians to follow.

My grandmother was a "picture bride." Her future relied on a simple snapshot of a man she did not yet know, an arranged marriage based on an exchange of photos, orchestrated by her family and his, in an alien land that she did not comprehend. The man in the photo was twenty years her elder, already an old man, broken by the long summer days of harvest with no escape from the beating sun. She sought a new life filled with hope. Yet fear and uncertainty lingered like haunting ghosts that accompanied her arrival. She did not understand the language of America.

When she arrived, my grandmother stepped into the searing one-hundred-degree heat of the farmlands surrounding Fresno, California. The green fields stretched for miles, the plush plantings required thousands of immigrants to hoe the weeds, to channel water to thirsty plants, to bend and snip the fruits. Their shovels scraped the parched earth, cutting the roots of weeds, clearing the land of unwanted pests. Slicing and abrading, grading and scouring, over and over, day after day. All this work for pennies. In fields with foreign crops they quickly learned to tend. The family took long, slow breaths. Not a race but a deliberate journey without end.

Strong backs were required for the grueling work that produced a rich bounty of fruits and vegetables. The Japanese, along with thousands of other immigrants, filled the countryside as farmworkers. Cheap labor was required to fulfill the demands of evolving modern agriculture and feed a nation's people who, in the early 1900s, were quickly fleeing rural America to new industrial jobs in cities. These new urban migrants wanted to forget where food came from. Leave the stoop labor to others.

As a young child, Shizuko will learn to step carefully in the soft, powdery dirt, another stride with her family as they complete another workday and a march towards some vague future of independence. She will leave footprints behind with a puff of dust in the arid soils. She feels safe and secure and free.

Working. Bearing harvests of family.
A hidden destiny awaits. Poor and colored.

4

The Foreign Language of Work

Shizuko speaks in Japanese for the first five years of her life until her illness, her separation, her departure.

Her family only communicates in Japanese. Her parents know little English, so their school-age children become their translators, interpreting in a foreign country for alien parents. Some phrases are impossible to decode in a new language in a land where immigrants are wanted mainly for their work in the fields, not for their spirits and words.

My family may have talked about Shizuko in front of me, but I did not realize it. Like many immigrant families, when a forbidden or closeted subject was raised and the parents "didn't want the kids to hear about it," one generation switched to another language. This was common in our household, family issues discussed in the open while some of us were blocked from garnering basic pieces of information. After a while, taboo subjects, since they were openly discussed, were no longer treated as unique and thus no longer special. And could be forgotten.

I grew up hearing Japanese but speaking very little. We knew words for foods like *gohan* for rice and *shoyu* for soy sauce and Buddhist holidays like *Hanamatsuri*, the birth of Lord Buddha, and *Ohigan*, the spring and fall equinox. I never had a conversation with my Baachans, or "grandmothers." They only spoke Japanese. That was one driving reason I left America to study in Japan for two years, studying abroad as a college exchange student. When I returned, I engaged with my grandmother Masumoto (both grandfathers had died before I was born). We talked about general things and had pleasant exchanges. But I now realize I didn't have some basic information. I overlooked events in a seemingly simple life, ignoring the major moments that define character. I was not curious. I missed opportunities. I was a fool.

Later, I conducted dozens of oral histories of neighboring Japanese American farm families. These interviews created a foundation for much of my writing and stories. I understood the role family played in many farm histories: the fragmentary accounts, the incomplete anecdotes, the restrained memories. A simple detail like a callused hand or a memory of the smell of rain on raisins could trigger hidden memories and the power of the unspoken. I can recall numerous times conversations ended in a penetrating sigh or grunt.

Yet I forget my own family had their own muted voices. The simple vocabulary and silences of everyday life opens the door into understanding experience. I now had to labor and find the language to make inquiries and try to translate the power of the unspoken. All the while my immigrant family seemed to be asking, "Is it OK to be me?"

Fresno and the surrounding small rural towns became home to thousands of Japanese immigrants. They ventured here mostly from two areas of Japan: Kumamoto and Hiroshima. This countryside was also filled with voices from many other countries and languages—Armenians, Italians, Portuguese, Germans, Chinese, Mexicans. They all sang the songs of work in the dirt. We all spoke "farm."

Growing up, I heard stories of Japanese voices chattering in the fields. A few English words blurred into conversations between the Issei, first-generation Japanese Americans. "Yes." "No." Then when a question was posed, with no clear answer, the classic immigrant's humor: "I no speak English."

Japanese country dialects told of the origins of my people. My father's parents spoke *Kumamoto-ben*, a rough tonal quality that seemed to match their reticent character. They added sounds to their words, demarking their space. Instead of *"genki"* which meant "healthy," they added *"genki bai."* *"Atsui"* or "hot" becomes *"atsuitai."*

Sometimes they used a different term, twisted to their common tongue. For good, instead of *"yoi"* or *"ii,"* you heard *"yoka-yoka."* Also, a phrase, *"batten,"* was occasionally tossed into the mix for no clear reason, often in the middle of a sentence. It roughly translated into "but" or "however," *batten* I never completely understood its usage.

Other Japanese immigrants laughed at these *inaka*, or country folks, from Kumamoto; they didn't understand some of these terms. It branded a family with an identity not to be forgotten. You could never escape the ghost of who you were and are.

But a common Japanese work chant lifted spirits and helped to pass the long hours. "*Yoisho*" is similar to English "heave-ho." "*Yoisho*" when lifting something heavy. "*Yoi-sho. Yoi-shooo,*" to summon extra muscle strength in a task. "*Yo-i-sho. Yo—ii—shooo,*" a call between two partners when passing a melon between field hands.

"*Yoo-ii-shooo.*" The heavy box was hoisted on to a wagon or truck. The tosser grunted to prepare the catcher. "*Yoo-ii-shooo.*" Timing was utmost importance as the stack grew and the effort had to be increased. At one point, the package flew free of all hands and unattached; "*shooooo*" accompanied the bundle as it soared independently, suspended midair for a moment until safely caught and stacked. "*Yoo-ii-shooo.*" Then it all repeated, over and over, all day long until the truck was filled.

And I never heard stories about complaining about their role as grunt laborers and farmhands. Their farm words will support and guide them in this new land.

But some sounds will forever remain foreign in America. A Buddhist chant, a haunting ring of a singing bowl, the deep tones of a gong. The vibrations echo as the harmonic tones ripple in the still air, familiar sounds of a spirit that brand the believers as aliens. Eternal. Hushed. Reticent. Shizuko will never speak the language of this new land. She will remain an immigrant. Restrained by her history. Silenced by a disability, yet she will find her own voice. And a Buddha lies quiet within her.

Foreign words
Growing
(dis)comfort food.

5

Landless—A Handful of Raisins

Shizuko grows up in a landless family. Japanese American immigrants are denied the right to purchase farms due to racist alien land laws of the 1920s. They continue to work in fields as laborers, especially during sweltering summers when thousands of hands are required to pick and bring in the harvest. They belong yet do not belong. They are destined to be aliens in a foreign land.

Shizuko is a Nisei, second-generation Japanese in America and an American citizen. That is what she is told and understands. By creating family, the immigrants hope the ghosts of ancestors will feel grounded, no longer alien, and they can explore this new world.

A cooling late summer breeze stirs the leaves; in the coming months they will change color and gently float to the earth, announcing the winds of change.

Is it a crime to be poor?

I try to picture Shizuko and the early years of my family in America. We were poor. We were not royalty or a privileged class escaping the homeland. No, we do not have samurai blood in our clan. My grandfathers were second sons, destined to inherit nothing and never groomed to take over their family rice plots. My grandmothers were older unwed women. I imagine their parents worried about who would take care of their daughters, so they arranged a convenient marriage for them. These women were tossed into an alien world across an ocean and yet hoped to escape the extreme poverty of a poor Japanese rice farm.

My family's story integrates a tale of escaping hardship and scarcity in search of something better. They left a homeland because they had few choices other than to journey to a foreign land filled with opportunity and hope and a destiny filled with misery and struggle. Dreams and doubt greeted them daily.

Poverty and disability are interwoven. To solve the mystery surrounding Shizuko, I reframe my thinking: money is one of the drivers of fate and destiny. To ignore this fact is to deny a basic fact in America—we are a land of both riches and wealth as well as destitution and pain. Yet disability need not be associated with deficiency; we impose cultural attitudes of discrimination as if it's a sin to be poor and wrong to be disabled. Instead, we unjustly use terms like "lower class," "handicapped," and "inferior."

In the late summer, like many Issei, my family harvests grapes for raisins. They follow the centuries-old tradition brought to California from Europe and the Middle East: green grapes are handpicked from vines and laid on trays which are placed on the ground in between the rows. The sweet morsels bake in the blazing sun. Gradually, over three to four weeks, the grapes shrivel and their skin curls and shrinks into fine wrinkles, a sign of a high-quality treat. They cure naturally and lay precariously in the open: vulnerable and exposed, helpless to face the whims of the weather. The farmers must trust nature like all ancestors who have worked the earth to grow food and life. A ritual of survival.

Each step in the process of making raisins requires an army of laborers. One vine can produce four to six pounds of raisins or from one to two tons of raisins per acre per year. Typically, that's about a thousand trays of grapes per acre; a small forty-acre farm could have up to 40,000 trays, each handpicked and sorted. Should the temperatures be cool, the trays need to be turned, flipped over so that the bottom side of each raisin bunch is rotated and exposed to the sunlight. If there's a threat of rain, back in the days when wooden trays were utilized, they were stacked to prevent the moisture falling on delicate half grape, half raisins, which are very vulnerable to rot and mold. Later, the same thousands of trays must be unstacked to once again bask in the sun. (Eventually paper replaced the wooden trays and with the threat of rain, they could be rolled to shelter the moist grapes, then unrolled once the threat passed.) Even in a normal year, the tons and tons of harvest need to be brought in, boxed in crates, and shipped to the nearby processing plants, such as Sun-Maid Raisins.

All this reflects how well the Issei fit in the fields: they are driven by a hunger. Both my paternal and maternal grandmothers work alongside their husbands.

As a team, they turn or stack wooden trays, filling boxes for the farmers they labor under. Monotonous work, days pile upon days. Their bodies are small and compact, a rare asset in this new land as they bend, crouch, squat and kneel for hours and hours in the dirt and dust.

Under five feet tall, my grandmothers toil repeatedly for weeks, answering the call for work with an unceasing drive. Neither their husbands nor themselves learn to speak English. They labor silently, hiding their emotions, concealing anger and fear. Never complete. All with the dream of planting themselves in the American soil they serve.

The Japanese fill the fields with strong backs to feed the country they cannot yet call home.

Aliens. The Issei must carry a registration card at all times branding them as foreigners.

Aliens. They cannot own property due to racist property land laws which specifically barred "Orientals" from land ownership (California Alien Land Law of 1913 and amended in 1920).

Aliens. They are destined to remain faceless, voiceless laborers working the fields. Invisible and hidden. Yet strangely protected and secure.

Their lives will fade with each passing season of work, leaving behind the ghosts of history. No songs celebrate their labor, no singing to cope with the drudgery and dreary conditions. Just the whispers of strangers. Take two steps forward, one step back.

After a long, long day of work, as the sun settles on the horizon and the temperatures shift from the brutal heat of day to the cooler forgiving night, Baachan Sugimoto, sits upright, staring to the west. She imagines that the sun is now settling upon her tiny native village in Japan.

Japan. The origin of the sun, the land of the rising sun. But for the Issei, Japan is the country of the setting sun. Their destiny is in this place far, far away.

For a moment, her muscles relax, and my grandmother turns her head, stretching aching neck muscles. She reaches upwards, extending her frame, spreading her arms, reaching for the sky. Inhale deep and hold. Then exhale as arms drop, bringing hands together. She is centered. Briefly. Fully. She prepares for a life of hardship and the immigrant's struggle to fit in, the perfect example of a Japanese term she often whispers: "*gaman*," to endure.

The summer slowly closes, and the harsh light gives way to the softer tones, the plants push their final round of pale leaves, one more attempt to grow life.

The leaves will soon fall, and pruning begins. Snip, snip. Slice, slice. Cut, cut. Each tree and each vine must be trimmed, sever weak limbs, sculpt a shape. Leaves will be shaken to the ground; they rustle when touched then silently float downward. Imagine them falling with a subtle thud when reunited with the earth. All part of the annual rite of passage to cut away the old in order to grow the future.

> *The families take their babies into the fields while they work. They rest the infants under a grapevine or peach tree, listening for their crying yet knowing there's little they can do since work must come first. Gradually, the children grow accustomed to the earth and amuse themselves. Playing games in the dirt, tossing clods, touching the earth. Studying the birds and insects for hours. Quietly, they grow content.*
>
> *Shizuko loves to lay on her back as she rests in an open field, witnessing an approaching cold front and clouds march across the overhead sky. The breezes gently shift branches with their cool air. Even the sunlight feels gentle. She gains the power to understand the forces of nature, like the wind. A lone yellow leaf breaks from the stem, floating and suspended in the air; twists and turns, gently riding the waves before settling on the earth. The forces that propel the leaf are not visible. She only hears and bears witness.*
>
> *Sounds of leaves. Falling and dancing. The wind—she can feel and hear. Shizuko can see the invisible. Shizuko learns to talk with nature.*

During the first wave of Japanese immigration to America, other immigrant groups from Europe settled in the San Joaquin Valley of California. Armenians litigated in federal immigration cases in 1909 and 1925. The courts ruled that they were "white Asians" and could therefore buy farmlands. Japanese were relegated to the fields and handfuls of raisins.

Japanese have a saying to cope with life's struggles: "Nana korobi ya oki;"
fall down seven times, get up eight . . ."

Guilty of wearing
the wrong faces
invisible in the fields.

PART TWO

SEPARATION
AND THE TIES THAT BIND

6

Diagnosis—A Child Forever Transformed

Shizuko, a five-year-old child in 1924. Disease attacks her brain, and her life will never be the same. It begins with sudden chills and a throbbing pain in her head. Then vomiting and a burning fever. No one knows what to do. Nothing wrong on the outside. No crushed hand. No broken, dangling leg. No blood or gash. It's all inside.

Meningitis changes lives in the blink of an eye. In just hours and days, the brain is enraged. Inflammation swells in the skull and spinal cord. The protective membranes fail and the head bulges from increased pressure of the fluid around the brain: the body turns against itself. Shizuko becomes confused, fuzzy, irritable, and difficult to comfort, traits that will linger for a lifetime.

No one calls the doctor. No emergency room visit. When your family is poor, rural, and classified as "aliens," you have few choices. You try to take care of your own, forge a path in your adopted country. You stumble and fall into the blackness of eternal night.

Shizuko's history is forever altered in that moment. A child transformed by a disease, a family altered and challenged by a different soul in their home. Shizuko survives yet must adapt to a world of few spoken words and unknowns. She now has to navigate a land of uncharted emotions, carrying a burden of a damaged brain, struggling to function in a world that will label her as deficient and trapped. She will not learn in the same way other children learn; she will grow in ways most others will not recognize. She will be falsely labeled a misfit and may never belong, publicly judged by inquisitional voices that wrongly condemn her. Unfairly separated: different, segregated, isolated, detached, apart, divorced. Enduring, her own survival will depend on an inner spirit. Her life will be different as her family, community, and country spin around her.

Shizuko is not alone. In America during the 1920s, tens of thousands of children die or are devastated by disease. Epidemics sweep through the countryside; sudden outbreaks are commonplace. Infectious diseases menace all populations, both in America and worldwide. As well as meningitis, scarlet fever, measles, tuberculosis, polio, and smallpox enter into the lives of families.

In the early 1900s, 30 percent of all deaths in America are children under five years old. In 1918, an influenza pandemic kills over 20 million people worldwide and 500,000 in America. If your child contracts meningitis in the early 1900s, 20–30 percent sustained permanent neurological damage. Brain injury and physical impairment are common.

Gradually, modern medicine experiments with antibiotics and vaccines, but the rural poor are the last to benefit from such breakthroughs. Meningitis outbreaks are greatly reduced in the 1920s with the introduction of penicillin. However, such treatments are slow to reach many. Isolated, invisible, and expendable—immigrant families are easily overlooked.

When you speak little or no English and toil silently in America's fields, far away from doctors, you are easily excluded. Add a foreign-looking face into the mix and combine that with a belief in a "pagan god," whole families are excluded from treatments and cures. The American lie turns its back to those who do not look right; certain lives have always mattered more than the lives of others.

The entire network of hospitals and medical care facilities, often attached to a Christian religious order, must have resembled a foreign land within the foreign country to immigrant communities. Rampant discrimination in healthcare are visible in segregated hospitals and uneven care. Yet many, like my family, willingly struggle to carve a niche for themselves in the country they have come to embrace.

The harsh realities of poor diets and bad living conditions stemming from poverty are at the root of many childhood illnesses, part of the landscape of numerous families crippled by diseases. Talk with most rural families and recreate a family tree of grandparents and great-grandparents. They will tell a tale of infant deaths, miscarriages, childhood farm accidents, and illnesses that left gaps in ages between siblings. Historical reality checks and milestones. A moment in the past that changes family forever—laden with buried secrets.

Yet a child with an intellectual disability weighs heavy on a family. They feel alone. They will be judged. A disease to be hidden by many in 1924. A burden to endure.

I remember writing my dad's obituary in 2010 and surrendering to tradition by including my mom's maiden name because it's part of a person's history and the family ties that bind us. That's how Ranee, a kind woman from Wildrose Funeral Home, found me; her initial phone call was followed by this letter:

Dear Mr. Masumoto,

I was contacted this morning in regards to Shizuko Sugimoto, who was born on October 13, 1919. I was able to research her birth record in the hopes of contacting family. I found that her mother's maiden name listed was Nomura. I found her as a child on the 1930 census along with her siblings. Her youngest sister was Yukino C. Sugimoto. I believe this youngest sister to be your mother.

Would you please contact me in regards to this? Central Valley Regional Center has been her payee for a number of years. Due to the poor condition of her health, she has been placed on Hospice Care at the Golden Living Center on A Street in Fresno. We believe that CVRC has set aside enough funds to take care of a cremation and burial of cremated remains. We would like to have the Buddhist priests come take care of the funeral rituals and after the cremation, place her cremated remains with other family buried in the area.

Thank you for assisting us. Please contact us whether or not your mother is her sister.

Sincerely,

Wildrose Chapel & Funeral Home

Before traveling to the funeral home, for a week I launch into a series of conversations with my mom. I refrain from sharing details of the phone call with my mother until I gather more information. No need to trouble my mom with a potential hoax but inquiring will cross a threshold by opening doors and wounds.

My mom remembers some details but adds, "Shizuko was much older than me, about eight years. So I don't remember that much. She kinda scared me." My mother then recounts some stories that she had learned from her older sister and brother, my aunt and uncle, "who remember much more."

I piece together parts of a tale, but no one has a complete story of Shizuko. Time blurs recollections and emotions obscure feelings. Historical facts clash with remembrances of things past. I grow uneasy by these gaps in memory, uncomfortable with the stories of poor health care, limited resources, restricted opportunities. The more details I learn, the more frustrated I grow, recognizing the seemingly simple things like a lack of a car or inability to speak English resulted in transformational moments and that things would never be the same.

This contributed to the fog of family history I explore. My family wore masks from the past. I now step into a bewildering path of what is remembered and forgotten.

One Memorial Day in the early 1960s, my mom dragged us kids to the Mountain View Cemetery in Fresno where the remains of her side of the family were housed. Once a year, the mausoleum for Japanese American families was opened and a service was held, not just for those who fought in the military but for all our families. The Sugimotos were there, ashes behind niche plaques organized in a neat row. Hundreds of other Japanese American families were represented in a similar fashion, small four-inch bronze squares attached to the wall, names emblazoned in gold. Families entered the small building and one by one, we bowed before the name plates and put our hands together in *gassho*, a Buddhist gesture of respect and gratitude. Most of the time, I kept my head tilted down and eyes lowered. When I was very young it felt creepy, the small room, cold and damp with ghosts of dead people surrounding me.

As the years passed, I grew more comfortable and began to study the walls of names. Some were so old the bronze plaques had aged. A few looked like they were made of wood, Japanese characters etched into the dark wood as a memorial to ancestors. I then realized there were three Sugimoto plaques, my grandfather, a space for Baachan Sugimoto (her plaque would be added in 1969), and two names of our clan I did not recognize. I had assumed they were distant relatives but then I noticed the dates: 1913–1925 on one and on the other, simply 1924.

These were the names of my ancestors, Japanese names of the dead.

Shigeru Sugimoto. Akiko Sugimoto. No one in our family had spoken about them yet their names lived forever next to my Jiichan, or "grandfather." These were names of "the other" children, my mom's siblings, my "other" aunt and uncle. These were common markers of lives taken early.

Shigeru, born in 1913 and died in 1925. As the eldest son, he was groomed and assumed the position as the "number one son" for over a decade and then had died.

A sister, Akiko, who died after three months of life. The starkness of a single year "1924" under her name. Life just beginning before ending.

They both passed more or less about the same time Shizuko had contracted meningitis, forever linking their deaths with her illness. Yet no one in the family remembers more. Stories I will never learn. Memories long ago locked away. Forgotten. The spirits had moved on.

I asked my mom about her siblings and she knew very little because they died before she was born. She then began to describe the hard, hard life of an immigrant family. My mom was born in 1927 and grew up during the Great Depression that began with the economic collapse of our nation (and the world) in 1929 and lasted until the beginning of World War II in 1942. I conjured images of starving families, poor hungry families, desperation and depression carved into the faces of children.

But my mom explained that country folk had gardens, even when our family lived on the edge of a small rural town, they had space to grow their own food. Besides, she added, how else would they have access to those fruits and vegetables from their homeland? Growing "their own food" was commonplace for most Japanese in America, even farmworker families (and many immigrant communities who longed for a taste of their native lands). My grandmother religiously planted her garden and like many Japanese American families, they filled their laundry rooms and garages with the distinct aroma of fermenting *tsukemono*, or "pickled vegetables."

Mom wrote me a list of their Great Depression diet: "We had rice for sure and lots of vegetables that our parents grew—especially daikon, napa, eggplant, cukes, and tomatoes. Very little meat—had tofu soy somen more but can't remember off the bat. Even in bad times we could always feed ourselves and feel secure."

Yet the family was poor, a stark contrast to the lush fields of produce they labored in. And like most of America, an ethic grew from the decade of limited resources, an attitude that often turned into an obsession to save everything.

In our home, we grew up with the term *"mottainai,"* or "don't be wasteful." A working-class ethic, *mottainai* became a mantra in our household. It was visible in our farm junk yard, where dad kept a stack of discarded but never forgotten old equipment, broken machine parts, and a repository of odd tools and implements. He truly believed he could use pieces from his pile for future repair work and innovative approaches to future jobs. And in many cases, he did—especially repairing farm equipment that I broke.

My mom was a conscientious and tidy hoarder. But unlike those whose mental condition was visible in the piles upon piles of stuff, she had her system of boxes, jars and envelopes scattered throughout the house. I discovered a jar bottle full of rubber bands, a cigar box full of paper clips, a large pickle jar full of match books, and of course the obligatory ball of string. She had another box of envelopes stuffed with two distinct collections: S&H Green Stamps and another collection of Blue Chip Stamps. (These were part of loyalty programs utilized mostly by grocery stores, a reward program for shoppers who collected these stamps to be redeemed for products in a catalog.)

"Don't be wasteful" translated into each and every meal, from scolding about filling your plate with so much food you couldn't possibly finish to subtly pawning off some of an entrée onto someone else's plate when you couldn't finish. Observing other non-Japanese families, I concluded this was not just cultural, it was an ethic that was carved into the psyche of an entire generation during one of the most challenging financial and emotional times in our modern history.

But Japanese Americans added a distinct cultural edict to their quest for thriftiness and frugality: shame. My immigrant grandmother would sometimes wiggle her index finger at me while shaking her head in an attempt to shame me into saving things and thereby save the family. My mom used the term "rescue" often as she fished out a discarded plastic fork that could be reused or a grocery bag that had a second life. We were decades ahead of the recycling movement, repurposing was a given in our home and farm. Being wasteful brought shame to our family.

Shizuko grew up during the Great Depression when hard times forced families to make hard decisions about care and resources. I read stories of families giving up their children, farming them out to relatives who could feed them, or some children became orphaned and separated from parents who could not care for them. The stories of those with disabilities were rarely recorded. Many were institutionalized and hidden. Shizuko embodies the stigma of a disability mixed with shame. She was "retarded," to use the common demeaning term of that era, which tragically caused embarrassment and unfounded humiliation. I wonder if a type of cruel guilt was mixed with a misguided dishonor that unfairly resulted in self-disgust and disgrace for the family. If the mantra of mottainai evolved in to a guiding principal for survival for an immigrant family desperately trying to carve a home in this new land called America, how could they determine what was "worth saving"?

But that's me talking today, in the present. I was not there and only have a few stories to reconstruct an entire misplaced life. Perhaps mottainai means not to waste a life, any and all lives.

Abandoned. Buried. Repressed. Unearthed. Revealed. Exposed.

7

The Assault

Shizuko alone. It's in the mid-1930s. The family leaves for work in the fields. The rest of the story remains vague, no one speaks about it. No details of the confusion and terror and pain.

No one, except possibly Shizuko, knows exactly what happened. She is a teenager, her body growing into a woman's, yet her mind remains injured because of the meningitis virus. "Bad neighbor boys" is one of the few phrases that is disclosed. White neighbor boys are paying too much attention to this Japanese American girl they perceive as impaired with a child's mind.

She is dragged. Unable to move. Clothes are ripped. A nightmare. No place to hide.

She is unable to explain. Her words were long ago mislaid in her brain. A vignette of chilling clarity. Or not. Perhaps her memory is repressed: does she pretend it didn't happen, buries the incident in order to cope in the present, a deep sleep that spills over her, a sleep like that of death? A darkness appears to save her.

Wildrose Chapel & Funeral Home. A stately old mansion, part of Fresno's original downtown homes for the wealthy and landed class. The structure was constructed in 1905 and had been converted into a funeral home by the 1990s. Ranee greets me, and we go upstairs for a conversation. She was occasionally given the paperwork to bury an individual who the county agencies were charged to care for and help with last rites and arrangements. Records showed Shizuko had no family responsible for her, no contacts to be notified with an impending death. Ranee was a devout Christian and has a calling to try and reach out so no one would be buried alone. She fanatically searches records and census reports for any surviving family members. In a true act of kindness, she hopes to locate someone related to Shizuko and stumbled on my mother's name. That's when I got the phone call.

Our conversation is warm, yet I am shrouded in confusion. I study the 1930 census record Ranee has uncovered and see all the names of my family, my grandparents, the uncles and aunts, my mom's name and yes, Shizuko. But I know all my uncles and aunts. Who is this woman? Or why has her family memory been erased? Is she indeed a lost aunt and not supposed to be found? Yet my feelings of indignation are misguided. I feel entangled in a perplexing history summarized by a simple phrase: it's complicated.

> *"She had an hourglass figure," my aunt explained. An hourglass figure, a phrase from an earlier era to describe the body shape of a woman, a bias of appearance focusing on the "ideal" construct of a woman's body. My aunt looked to the side and quietly continued, "She attracted too much attention."*
>
> *No details were then provided. Baachan Sugimoto blamed herself for the incident. Did she neglect Shizuko? Was she a bad parent?*
>
> *A simple story followed. Baachan Sugimoto held Shizuko closely and reached for a pair of scissors. She held onto fistfuls of black hair and began to chop off clumps. She wanted Shizuko to look like a boy. Hack, mangle, prune. Cut the hair short, uneven, rough. Make her look like a boy. Simple and symbolic. Then she could be safe. Snip and trim. Maybe those "bad neighbor boys" would now leave her alone.*

What happened to Shizuko was tragic and horrific. There remains a sense that the past is past. No one can or is willing to corroborate the details of the act and the response.

But it's easy to judge the history based on today's standards and proclaim that my family's response was timid and weak. In this confusion, I'm guilty of conjecture, wanting to probe a hidden and buried memory. I should protect my family's privacy and cloaked history because I cannot comprehend the startling circumstances of that moment in time. Leave the past behind. Let go. It's done. Let sleeping demons sleep. Don't cross that threshold. Let the ghosts be ghostly.

Contrast my family's response to today's first-person exposés and the over-sharing of often dark, extremely personal and numbing confessional impulses circulated as anecdotes. I fear that the most riveting and revealing story to share about Shizuko was actually the worst thing that happened to her—a performance of pain I exploit in order to draw attention to my family's story and plight. Yet, what about the boys? We ignore the fact that the "bad neighbor boys" were allowed to keep their secrets secret. My family was powerless to do anything more. If I were present back then, I too may have accepted my own impotency.

In a single moment, shame pierces my family's history and legacy. It lives in the body, sinks into the ground, fuses with race and poverty. Shame morphs into a crime centered upon Shizuko and she is both wronged and branded as disgraced. She carries the stigma of dishonor, and the family is humiliated because of their powerlessness.

Yet I cannot change the past and only learn of family history in fragments with guarded emotions. I cannot begin to comprehend this tragedy. What's missing is self-awareness: memories can be prisons and I wrongly disregard context. You learn to live with incomplete stories and a silence that echoes with each haunting question and unresolved answer. A respect for what you don't know, a search for a past I can never totally claim. A harsh reality—some family secrets are destined to remain secret.

Silent suffering.

8

Temples

Jiichan Sugimoto crafts replicas of Japanese temples and pagodas. Shizuko quietly plays in this recreated Land of the Rising Sun. No one judges her here, she is shielded and protected to be herself by herself. The wooden structures are her height, detailed and specific, made from memory and a carpenter's eye for detail. Shizuko can walk free and alone in this garden, breathe in the aroma of freshly cut and shaved wood. It's OK for her to be herself in this wonderful tranquil world, even if for a moment.

She wanders from a pagoda to a temple. She skips and swings her arms. At times, she performs a dance move, Tankō Bushi, the coal miners' dance at Obon, a Japanese summer festival to honor ancestors. She mimics the clap. Cho-chon-ga-chon. Step as arms swing down to one side. Dig, dig. Hands open, palms upright. Once, twice. Toss over shoulder or carry your shovel. Each side. Wipe the sweat from your forehead as you step back. Then the other side. Push, push. Clap hands. Repeat. Shizuko can dance.

The elaborate wooden models are sheltered in their front yard. As a small tree loses its leaves with the first autumn chill, yellow and orange float from the limbs and collect on the craftsman's art. They capture a sense of time passing, a changing season. The assortment of structures creates the illusion of Japan. Here Shizuko and her father can escape and find shelter and hide momentarily from the problem.

I leave Wildrose with more questions than when I had arrived. I will visit this person called Shizuko to verify her existence and somehow make a determination if she is indeed family. But I have no photograph of her as a child, no image of her growing up. There are no memories that are passed down, no stories allowing us to engage with history and make it feel real. Learning about Shizuko demands that I inquire about the history of the people we carry inside us, the family stories that came before me.

There remains a few accounts about my grandfather and his woodworking skills. I recall a single photograph with my other aunt, Lorada, as she poses in the recreated temple garden of my grandfather. Lorada is closest to Shizuko in age and I'm told she often took care of her. The highly detailed miniature structures brought his homeland back to my grandfather. It replaced the farm he could never own, the place he and his family could escape to and find a moment of solace: an inner cave for aliens and misfits and a threshold to a special protected space.

Days after the bombing of Pearl Harbor in 1941, rumors spread of evil "fifth-column or sabotage activities" that contributed to the "sneak attack" by the Japanese. Supposed accounts from Hawaii described treasonous evidence such as "directing arrows that were discovered cut in sugar cane fields" to help Japanese pilots locate their targets. Another story supposedly documented one of the few Japanese pilots who was shot down was "wearing a Hawaiian high-school ring and was carrying Honolulu streetcar tokens."

Caught in a whirlwind of hysteria, my family tried to respond to prove themselves as Americans. My Masumoto grandparents heeded the suggestion made by Japanese American organizations to buy US Savings Bonds to prove their patriotism. They purchased one valued at fifty dollars and they kept it for decades.

My mom, a freshman in high school, volunteered to join the "Skywatch Program," a citizen group that was part of the "Ground Observer Corps" and tasked to watch the sky for enemy aircraft intent on attacking the United States. She was paired with a Caucasian high school senior and instructed to keep a lookout for aircraft based on a pamphlet identifying "friend or foe" aircraft.

The temple gardens would be one of the first things destroyed once the Sugimotos departed. The wooden models were seen as symbols of the "evil" America was fighting against. They did not belong in a small rural California farm town, just as these "evil" people who were to be imprisoned for the acts of their fore-fathers. The pagodas and shrines my grandfather had created and built were symbols of his love of his homeland. But they were also perceived as a type of ancestor worship—an allegiance to Japan and her pagan gods.

The gardens would be burned. Enraged Americans fought the enemy in their backyard, igniting the wooden structures, incinerating them from their existence. Americans sought to cleanse themselves from the enemy evil empire. Ironically, this cremation left ashes that would forever be part of the earth.

The Skywatch volunteers did not need to look far for signs of the enemy. They could look at my mom's face or see Shizuko skipping in her garden and find their nemesis.

Temples of a home never to return.
How does it feel to be defined as the problem?
To become American.

PART THREE

PRISON

9

The Taking and The Promise

Shizuko, at the age of twenty-three, lives with an intellectual disability. Many label her as lost and condemned. She will struggle and fight in a war of survival, stumbling and searching. Soon she will relearn the lessons of separation.

The family stands in silence. December 7, 1941. Bombs are dropped by the Japanese military on Pearl Harbor. The United States declares war against Germany and Japan. A moment in history that alters the course of Japanese Americans forever. Their rights are gradually stripped away, restrictions unfold like a never-ending nightmare. A hundred thousand faces transformed in America overnight: they now carry the masks of the enemy. They are helpless to respond, unable to initiate action, powerless to assert control over their lives. All purpose in life evaporates with the stroke of a pen when Executive Order 9066 is signed by the President who decides who gets to be American. Part of the lies agreed upon.

The Issei feel betrayed, the country they had adopted turns its back to these immigrants. The young Nisei, who were only teenagers, are thrust into a new role: heads of households because they speak English. By the summer of 1942, over 110,000 Americans of Japanese descent, many American citizens, were incarcerated and relocated to evacuation centers scattered across desolate areas of the United States, ranging from Jerome, Arkansas, to Heart Mountain, Wyoming.

Confusion. Pain. Racism. Slurs. Hatred. Rounded up and put into prison, adults, grandparents, and even children who are born in America and citizens. A people uprooted, forced to sell possessions and property and leave behind a life. They are instructed to bring one suitcase; it's all they are allowed to carry.

They board trains for unknown places behind barbed wire. For many, especially Issei men, their life ends as their families are forever torn from the land they had hoped to call home.

The Sugimoto family is ordered to evacuate to a distant and unknown place called Gila River Relocation center in the desert south of Phoenix, Arizona. No one knows how long they will be imprisoned. No one knows if they will ever return. No one knows what to expect. Mass incarceration. The shame of confinement.

The situation: Shizuko's father is dying of stomach cancer. He is gravely ill and there is little or no treatment for a poor immigrant, especially during the hysteria following the declaration of war against his native country. What options are available? Leave him behind? Take him to unknown destinations? No one knows how they will travel nor how long nor what care will be provided during the journey. And what to do with Shizuko? Will there be care for Shizuko while in custody? What hope does she have to survive this odyssey? These issues tested our family.

Shizuko wanders in her father's Japanese gardens. She slips into another world, another reality, walking the familiar paths, bare feet touching the soil, hands reach out and stroke the flowers and green leaves, fingertips gently stroke and feel the familiar wood carvings. A breeze stirs the dry parched earth, and a puff of dust is kicked up. She escapes on her own farm walk. Breathe in the scent of home, familiar and safe. The summer sun warms the land, hot August days the skin knows well. Embrace the sweat of the known before the unknown will reshape memories forever. How would Shizuko describe herself and her world that would soon be turned upside down?

I see this moment in my family's history in black and white images. Men and women in gray with long faces of confusion. Children standing alone with a helpless look of silent fear. Soldiers in drab uniforms, they look dark in my vision of the past. Everyone looks barren.

My family will ride darkened trains into the desert. Shades drawn over the windows, it's unclear who makes such an order. To shroud the evacuees in secrecy and conceal the path to their destination? Or somehow protect them from scrutiny and supposedly shield them "for their own good"? This makes no sense to me. Pandemonium. Turmoil. Confusion. Chaos reigns.

They will be greeted by a dry, parched wind in the lifeless Arizona desert. It howls over the grim and naked landscape. A harsh chill rises from the starkness of an alien place, foreign, strange, remote, lifeless. The mountains surround the camp with dark brown shadows. The occasional shrub clings to the barren clay squeezed between rocky rubble. The dirt is parched, cracked and bare. Shabbily constructed barracks that they are forced to call home, four families sharing a single wooden structure with nothing to divide stranger from stranger, cell mate from cell mate. Loose wood bangs with the wind. Dust is kicked up and blinds. A people are again branded as misfits and unwanted. Adrift in a wilderness. The sound of emptiness permeates the land and the soul. A forsaken place for the forsaken.

Voices are muffled. The cries first echo throughout these desolate and fabricated cities of 10,000 in the middle of nowhere. But the sounds quickly terminate. No one is listening.

It is a sin to be Japanese American in 1942. Anger. Fear. Hysteria. Lies. Hostility. Why doesn't my family resist? Forces beyond their control rule over their lives. In a single moment, their world turns upside down. They lose everything, families are separated, lives are forever torn. I try to shed light into this dark episode and the only images appear as bleak photographs. Silently, a people internalize the shame. I can't change history, but I can try to understand the meaning—"their" meaning—of *shikata ga nai*, or "it can't be helped."

I was told the story of their departure. Oniisan, or "oldest brother"—my Uncle Mas, who was the eldest child—was forced to try and take care of everything. His closest brother, Uncle Ted, was trapped in the US Army, drafted right before the bombing of Pearl Harbor. Ted wrote letters about a handful of other Japanese American soldiers who had been also separated from the other troops during basic training, guns taken away, trapped in limbo while serving a country that no longer trusted them.

The family only had a few weeks to prepare for evacuation, knowing they might never be allowed to return. For many in the Fresno area, the final exile orders were issued in August, just weeks before farmers were to pick grapes for raisins. The Masumoto family was renting a vineyard, grapes were growing fat in the summer sun, a year's worth of labor about to be harvested. My dad talked with the landowner, a white widow who was worried, not about our family's imminent departure but rather who would pick the grapes. She was not alone; hundreds of other farmers would miss the Japanese Americans as grape pickers. So Fresno farm groups sent letters to politicians and local newspapers requesting to delay relocation until after the raisin crop was harvested, then the government could continue the expulsion.

My father, with few options, struck a deal with the landowner. Our family would get pennies on the dollar for a crop about to be reaped. (To add insult to the injury, during the war years, the government supported a much higher price for raisins. The sweet, dried fruits were often used in K-rations for soldiers fighting overseas. The return for a ton of raisins was double the rate as opposed to the low prices during the Great Depression.)

A week before evacuation, our family was kicked out of the farmhouse that was on their rented property. The landlord wanted to welcome the new renters who would harvest her raisins and let them move in as soon as possible. My father was furious. In an act of private civil disobedience, he moved our family to a nearby barn where a kind neighbor farmer allowed them to stay for a few days. He then proceeded to toss out all of their processions from the rented house that they could not take with them. He piled tables, chairs, furniture, clothes, dishes, cups, pots and pans into a heap and set fire to them in a final act of defiance, his personal protest.

The Sugimoto family tried to store some family possessions and left behind much. My grandfather had built an extensive Japanese garden with multiple hand-carved miniature wooden structures, recreations of temples and tea houses from Hiroshima. His work would be abandoned. The family joked, good thing they were poor farmworkers and didn't have to sell a farm out of desperation.

But two challenges loomed for my Uncle Mas.

First, his father—my grandfather—was very sick with stomach cancer. He didn't have long to live. Would the internment centers have a hospital and doctors? And a crematory?

Second, my grandmother was worried about Shizuko. She had been a challenge to take care of at home. What did a concentration camp have in store for a child with an intellectual disability? Shizuko was in her early twenties, still tiny and petite, with limited yet unique and often misunderstood communication skills. Home in their small rural town had now become a wasteland for refugees. The unknowns dominated the future. Unable to speak English, with her husband on his deathbed, my grandmother pleaded for her oldest son, my Uncle Mas, to seek for help from anyone.

A few days before the family was to depart on trains for Arizona, a county sheriff arrived at the door. An agreement was made: the authorities would take Shizuko and she would become a "ward of the state."

When I first heard this story, I had an image of big white men tearing Shizuko from the arms of her family, dragging her to their police car and whisking her away. Terror and confusion reigned, the dark human tragedies of a refugee family trapped in the madness of war. But an aunt corrected me. She said Uncle Mas had invited the authorities to come. No official governmental policies had been established and everyone would try to help as best they could.

My aunt explained that it was "so very hard." Shizuko clung to my grandmother, refusing to let go; she was afraid of these strangers. My grandmother wept as the men guided Shizuko away, into the car.

Over and over, Shizuko cried out one of the few words she could mouth, "Mama . . . Mama . . . Mama."

Then my grandmother pulled Uncle Mas aside and made a request: ask the authorities for a promise. "*Yakusoku*," she said. Promise. Then added, "Make them vow that they will take care of Shizuko. Make them agree to this obligation. *Yakusoku o suru.*" Honor the promise.

The request was made. The authorities quietly nodded their heads. They affirmed their conviction.

My uncle returned to reassure my grandmother. He said the authorities swore they'd take care of Shizuko. They would honor their promise. "*Yakusoku o mamoru*"—they vowed to "protect the promise."

The same government that was imprisoning my family and uprooting tens of thousands was now promising to take care of my aunt with her disability.

I am confused. I don't know what I would have done in those circumstances. I cannot feel all the complex emotions of that moment. Letting go out of love and a hope for a better life: the paradox twists my sense of history and right versus wrong. I dare not pause to conjecture on the darkness which lies behind my family's hidden stories, protecting me and my generation. Too many questions, too few answers. Stop asking, the ancestors tell me: accept vulnerability to free yourself from victimization.

During the journey to Arizona, the train stopped in Los Angeles where officials tried to remove my grandfather and take him to a medical facility. But he refused, demanded to stay on the train, gripping the train seat with all the energy his frail body could muster. He would not be separated from family. Within a month at Gila River, he died. He was the first to pass away in "camp." The authorities didn't know what to do. They allowed the family to take the body to a nearby crematory in a small town where a service was held. My uncle said at least the last rites were not conducted behind barbed wire and he was glad the relocation camp did not have a crematory in their initial design plans.

They became ghosts in this land of the undead.
Forces beyond their control ruled over their lives.
They lost everything, families separated, lives torn.
Silently, internalizing the burden.

10

Bedlam

Shizuko is assigned to numerous institutions from 1942 to the early 1950s. We have no record of where nor who took care of her and it is impossible to know what it was like for her, whether there was any kindness or reliability in her world or whether it was as bleak as I imagine it might have been.

Unknown treatments, ambiguous supervision, nameless custody. She is adrift in a maze of facilities. The descent must have been dark. She is swallowed into an alien world. Plunged into a pit of pain and sorrow, a blackness of eternal night. Care is lacking for mental patients in prior decades. A dungeon. Compounded by the war and scarce resources. Stumbling. Add her Japanese face and name to the subterranean pool. The pain must have been overwhelming . . . or not. Perhaps she learns not to feel and not to think: a vacancy fills her mind in order to survive. The closing walls press without resistance. She has little control over her circumstances.

Life magazine publishes an explosive article and photo essay entitled "Bed-lam, 1946," which uncovers the hidden calamity and debacle within mental institutions in America. It exposes the terrible conditions stating that "most U.S. mental hospitals are a shame and disgrace." Horrific black-and-white photos. Imagines of patients abandoned, sleeping on floors. Stories of abuse. Mental patients housed in asylums, packed into facilities with hordes of others. Restraints. Soiled robes. Naked bodies. Locked up. Forgotten in an America that hides: a deliberate attempt to camouflage the facts of history.

The walking dead. Guilty of being who they are. Shizuko becomes a ghost and slips into the land of the undead.

Evacuation. Internment. Relocation. Those are the terms I occasionally heard while growing up about the World War II confinement of Japanese Americans because they looked like the enemy. Every once in a while, my folks mention "camp"—they refer to their penitentiary as either internment centers or most commonly "camp." I hear them talk about neighbors who are from "Block 23" or "Block 24." Our family is imprisoned in Gila River Relocation Center (one of the ten relocation centers constructed by the US government and scattered across desolate areas of the American landscape). Block 23 for the Masumotos. Block 24 for the Sugimotos. For four years, this is our family home, shared with 10,000 other inmates, behind barbed wire and armed guards. Abandoned. Insignificant. Forsaken.

Families partition a barrack with strangers, blankets are hung to divide the living quarters. My mom describes the habit of shaking her clothes before putting them on; otherwise, a scorpion may be caught in a pant leg. Because dust storms blow across the open plain surrounding them, they must stuff paper and rags in between the wall cracks to keep the dirt particles from piling up inside.

The harsh landscape creeps into their barracks. No one knows the next month's weather or what the next season will cast upon daily life. They have no history here. They are tossed into an abyss of unknowns. Trapped.

They call it a "block," not cell. They label it "camp," not jail. They designate it a "center," not prison. I grow confused and infuriated. As I learn more, I wonder why they didn't protest? What could have been done? Do I have the right to question? These walls do not speak. I cannot hear the voices of my family.

A family member whispers: "*Gaman*. This is just one more test we must endure."

My parents and grandmothers often utilized the word *gaman*, which translates as "to endure" or "persevere." When we had to labor through a long harvest day picking peaches in 105-degree heat, I'd hear them say *gaman* as motivation. During my elementary school days, when I had a lot of homework and struggled through math problems, my mom encouraged me to work through it all—with a gentle reminder of that term. It was our path to success.

Once my mom and I visited my uncle (my mom's brother) at the Veteran's Hospital in Los Angeles. He scared me with his frightening language and angry temperament. He constantly swore at his roommate, snapped at the staff, and seemed as if he did not want to see us. My mom explained that he was bitter after his stroke. He had been drafted into the US Army before Pearl Harbor, treated terribly during basic training when the military didn't know how to handle men who looked like foreigners. He then joined the 442nd infantry battalion and was wounded fighting for the country that imprisoned his family. He blamed the wartime injury—shrapnel to the brain that was unable to be removed—for his stroke. He resented the circumstances of his condition and grew frustrated with his disability. Life was unfair. He cursed at his roommate with brutal wounds that would never heal. Yet my mom insisted on *gaman*—we all should accept what life throws at us.

The 442nd had adopted the motto "Go For Broke," derived from the gambling term "to fight for the big win." They engaged in two wars: against the Germans in Europe and the struggle to fight racial prejudice in America. This regimental combat team became the most decorated unit for its size and length of service in the entire history of the US military. They adopted the language of survival by proving themselves and putting everything on the line while also carrying deep personal wounds.

My uncle had a right to be frustrated and mad. I would have been too. He had faced challenges and tests only to be dealt another trial and crushing verdict.

What business had he with hope? The world remained dark. His past history was hidden. I dare not pause to conjecture on this past. A darkness lay behind this veteran.

Only in college did I learn much more about Japanese American history and especially about relocation and internment. I thought about my family and why they didn't stand up for their rights and protest. I read stories of those who did—Gordon Hirabayashi, Minoru Yasui, and Fred Korematsu—who challenged internment in 1942. Initially, the court cases sided with the US government, however, decades later they were later overturned and deemed a misjudgment.

I also learned of individuals who refused to be drafted in 1944: the infamous Heart Mountain resisters. When the military questioned if eligible men would be willing to serve in the US military, this group refused and were arrested. The Japanese American community labeled them with a pejorative term: the "No-No Boys" because they answered "no" on the two important questions:

Question 27: Are you willing to serve in the armed forces of the United States on combat duty wherever ordered?

Question 28: Will you swear unqualified allegiance to the United States of America and faithfully defend the United States from any or all attack by foreign or domestic forces, and forswear any form of allegiance or obedience to the Japanese emperor, to any other foreign government, power of organization?

(Yet my dad was one of those men drafted into the army and he served, arriving in Europe just as the war was ending.)

Many others had demonstrated in the relocation centers. The outspoken critics were then rounded up and placed in Tule Lake Internment Camp in the mountains of Northern California, which became home to those deemed disloyal and untrustworthy.

The majority accepted their fate. Like my family, they felt helpless, forced into compliance. "What could we do?" my father lamented to me during one of our few moments he was willing to discuss internment.

Could *gaman* be a sign of weakness? In America, you fight for what you believe in, protest inequality, battle when wronged. If you don't stand up for yourself, no one would respect you. Was I part of a meek and quiet people?

But would I have fought back? A huge burden was thrust upon my father during internment: the obligation to take care of the family. The number one son, his older brother, had been drafted into the army before Pearl Harbor. He fought two wars, much like my mom's brother. For my father, the incarceration unfolded as a family affair, not simply a violation of the individual.

During 1942, the erosion of rights was gradual, beginning with curfews and restricted travel for Japanese Americans. During the winter chill, boundaries were drawn, initially along coastal areas and gradually moving inland. In the spring, it was OK to be Japanese east of Highway 99, a main north–south thoroughfare dividing California in two. Those living west of this dividing line were deemed dangerous and incarcerated in assembly centers, often isolated at county fair grounds and horse racing tracks. Then by August, it was decided all Japanese Americans on the West Coast had to be confined, despite the fact that in the eight months from December 7, 1941, to the boarding of trains in August 1942, not a single serious act of espionage or sabotage was committed by any Japanese American descendant in the United States. This slow dismantling of rights may have beaten a people into submission.

The wind blows cold and then howls over the barren landscape. Hastily constructed wooden barracks. Loose wooden boards bang with the wind. Barbed wire fences and stockade walls. Guard towers with armed soldiers. The sound of emptiness permeates the land and the soul.

Distant mountains on the horizon spread like a wall separating all from freedom. Occasional storm clouds rolled in, a wave across the vista, teasing all with a chance of rain, but most often no drops fell: this was a desert, parched and empty.

Worst of all, no one knew how long their sentence was.

Prisoners without a trial. Guilty of enduring a face that looked like the enemy. Americans convicted of being the wrong American.

Why? What did they do? How long is their punishment? The answers are trapped in the darkness of their prison. They are bound together by the faces they wear: the masks of strangers. They ask: "Does anyone know we're here?"

These prisons were scattered throughout the remote and desolate regions of the western United States. Americans of Japanese descent. They walked on the coarse dirt of the Arizona desert. They limped through the snows of Arkansas. They wandered in the highlands of Wyoming and Idaho. Places on the map no one knew before and now they must accept and adapt. They had no control over their lives.

Lifeless in the desert. A winter breeze chills their bones. A high fence encloses the compound, towers with guns pointed inwards. But where would you escape to? Nothing for miles and miles. Alone in this prison because we look Japanese, because we look like outsiders.

Marked as misfits in a wilderness.

It's easy to imagine from the present and ignore the emotions of that moment in time when larger forces could not be ignored: obligation, duty, and yes, *gaman,* translates into a type of acceptance.

> *During these dark years, does Shizuko also carry* gaman *within her? She has been missing, her life filled with pain and shame. She too finds the strength to endure. Yet there will be no redress for her.*

Isolated. Trapped. Abandoned.
Accepting vulnerability.
Shikata ga nai. It can't be helped.

II

Faces We Wear—The Mongoloid Idiot

Her family is taken away, Shizuko is considered a burden. Her disability is seen as a crime by others and thus, she is condemned to the wilderness. Appalling "Ugly Laws" are passed in parts of the country making it unlawful for those with "unsightly or disgusting characteristics" to be allowed in public ways or places or exposed in public view.

An ironic and bittersweet twist: Shizuko could have possibly experienced better care while institutionalized during World War II because she is mistakenly identified as a "Mongoloid Idiot." Mongoloid idiot: an atrocious and derogatory term used to refer to the mental deficiency now more commonly referred to as Down syndrome. Shizuko does not wear the face of the enemy "Jap" during the war but is brutally considered a retarded misfit whose disease makes her look Asian.

During World War II, the ranks of the people with disabilities swell as more and more families give up their children and the nation gears up for war. At the same time, many workers in these mental units and hospitals are drawn away to fight in the war. Yet Shizuko may have found comfort with a new wave of attendants in these institutions: conscientious objectors who refused to fight in war for ethical reasons. They chose to march to a different drum. They are readily employed to help fill the ranks and became the new family for Shizuko. In a twist of fate, some of these new workers also seek to expose the horrors of neglect within the walls of these institutions and advocate for the rights of the incarcerated. Shizuko begins her journey of finding and building allies.

The faces we wear. Shizuko could not change hers. It may have helped. My family could not change theirs and they were convicted and imprisoned.

The faces we wear and accompanying prejudices—exposed during the war. *Time* and *Life* magazine in 1942 ran stories "How to Tell a Jap" and described the features of the enemy Japanese versus other "friendly" Asians like Chinese. We believe to have evolved as a nation, striving for a colorblind world where we do not judge by appearance or physical features. But in America, race still matters and translates into masks we are assigned no matter our true faces underneath. We are forced to march in a parade of history based on the color of our skin.

The families missed their homes, the earth they once worked, the tools that connected them. They missed their shovels. A simple implement, metal and wood. They reimagined the feel of their daily instruments of life. Over the years, the blade of a favorite shovel had worn from a point to a curved shape, honed by the sandy loam dirt, abraded by the countless hours and hours of purging weeds. The handle was smooth and cool to touch, oiled by hands working it over and over, gliding in the parched dirt, digging out the shallow roots, But the blade also measured time, ever so gradually eroded by the labor of working hands, each decade grinding the metal another inch and then another. They could feel time—the past in the present. With luck, they could imagine a future. Imagining another fate was their ally, nurturing a sense of identity by not what they had but what they missed.

Memories of home, of work, of action dance in their minds. While imagining their shovels, their bodies begin to sway, arms swing and mimic the motion of "shovel work."

It reminded them of a Japanese summer festival called *Obon* and the upbeat music of one song called "*Tankō Bushi*," commonly referred to as the "Coal Miners' Song" in which dance movements depict work in mines mimicking shoveling coal, throwing a bag of coal over the shoulders (some refer to this motion as carrying your shovel), wiping sweat from the brow and pushing a cart of coal. The footsteps and motions of this simple folk dance and song included a repetitive motion—clap, dig, toss, sweat, push, clap, and repeat—a repetitive series of actions and a joyous moment in order to endure work.

The same motions Shizuko dances with hundreds of miles away.

The interned Japanese Americans were alone. All they had were their memories dancing in their imagination when their masks were purged.

Unmasked illusions
of how to endure
with the faces we wear.

12

Camp Gardens

In her own domain, Shizuko adapts by constantly being in motion and walking. She wanders, as if recreating her childhood by imagining a walk in the fields where her parents once labored. Or she drifts between the wooden sculptures her father had once created in their concealed garden. Shizuko constructs an internal world to become a placed person—someone to be seen. Shizuko endures her own universe as a castaway.

When I returned to our family farm after graduate school, I began collecting oral histories. I interviewed not only my family but also our farming neighbors. I listened as stories were shared and began to understand the gaps in their answers, the times when quiet filled the room and left blank moments on my tape recorder. The silence told a story, a moving narrative like a mystery for me to decipher and accept.

Shame played a role. Japanese Americans felt humiliated and betrayed by their country. But many internalized their wounds and began to blame themselves. My family embodied a culture of group behavior, trust in the authorities. My grandparents, Issei, who legally immigrated to America, grew old and dependent on English speaking children. My parents, Nisei, felt powerless to fight. I believe they somehow felt responsible, slipping into a psyche of detachment and avoidance, much like a social amnesia: their posttraumatic response to suppress unpleasant memories. For Nisei, to be American was to be accepted.

For my peers, the Sansei, third-generation Japanese American, we face a gap in our personal histories. Our parents didn't talk about the internment. We know it happened but rarely heard stories. We grew up ignorant or sometimes ignoring the fact our grandparents, parents, aunts, and uncles were prisoners.

We detached our connection with the ghosts of our forebears, surrendering a link with our immigrant selves.

Shards of stories. Fragments of yesterdays. Intentionally forgotten emotions. Scraps of memories. These are all we had to build an identity. Who am I? Not Japanese. American, but how? For immigrants, to become American calls for you to forget.

The Masumoto and Sugimoto families live for years behind barbed wire in the Arizona desert. Hatsujiro, Shizuko's father, is one of the first internees to die in the relocation camps. Masa, Shizuko's mother, is now a single parent, struggling to keep the family together. In this prison setting, families begin to eat separately in the mess hall. Teenagers jump from mess hall to mess hall to be with friends. Young adults gather at their own tables. Even the Issei congregate by themselves, speaking exclusively in their native tongue, carving *hashi* or chopsticks from the sage brush collected from outside the walls.

In an act of resilience, not resistance, after the first years of captivity, many residents plan and build gardens, attempting to humanize their cells and assert limited control over the immediate conditions of their isolation. When possible, they dig and pour cement to make fishponds that wind their way around walkways and barrack foundations. They seek to find some purpose and meaning in the depths of their separation and confinement.

These monuments survive the decades. During a visit in the 1970s, I journeyed back to Gila River and discovered such remains. The wooden barracks had long ago been removed in an attempt to wipe away this black mark in American history. But some relics, such as the abandoned fishponds, survived. Some even held water from the infrequent rainstorm in this arid climate. I uncovered the cement steps and garden entries that had the carved initials of their creators embedded in the cement surface, like a headstone. These physical relics carried emotions and meaning, perhaps because I too work the earth, I could feel with empathy.

My mom, like many Nisei, grew up amidst this cruel reality: she didn't know any better. She was fourteen years old when the uprooting unfolded. Though young, she spoke English, which her aging parents did not. She was forced to translate all which was unfolding and attempt to process the meaning of racism against her people. Her brothers were drafted and ironically fought for freedom in Europe and the Pacific while the family remained confined. Other siblings left camp to escape when free zones opened east of the Mississippi. At such a young age, she held the family together, the daily beat of a drum and the burden to carry: to keep the family as one. A spiritual calling. A crusade. Even as the family separated.

Yet my mother also witnessed glimpses of a new life: she went to school with other Nisei; she socialized, attended gatherings, walked in a high school graduation during these years of imprisonment. The sounds of normal—a school dance, a baseball game, making crafts and art—fused with the barren landscape. She remembers capturing the moment by humming Louis Armstrong's "On the Sunny Side of the Street." (I wonder what she thought of another Armstrong hit he later released: "What Did I Do to be So Black and Blue." Before marrying my father and returning to farming, my mom spent a few years in Los Angeles after the war and vividly recalled going numerous times to the Santa Monica Pier to see Armstrong perform live.)

A Nisei neighbor told me a story about getting a package sent from California. She too was at Gila River Relocation Center, trapped in the desert, anxious to hear about their family farm in California. She opened the box and inside were pomegranates, red, juicy, and luscious. They were from a tree back home, picked by a kind neighbor, shared with their rightful owners. She and her family cracked open the plump fruit, peeled back the layers of brilliant seeds and slowly ate each one, crunching them with their teeth. Red juice squirted out and stained hands, fingers, and lips. She told me of a bittersweet taste of home that filled her mouth as she imagined their lone tree in their distant garden. That sensation burst open with each crunch, a memory born of places you never should leave.

They will forever live with these ghosts of hate and incarceration. Internalized. Captives. They lose years of their life behind bars, convicted of being who they are. They cannot unsee this prison. Their history will hold them hostage. Alone in the Arizona desert, they find patches of sun to stand and bathe in the light with the hope to face challenges and one day to be seen. In the moonlight of a clear night sky, they can cast a shadow of their apparations.

What could you have done?
To right a wrong. Stand up. Little to lose.
Or blame ourselves?
Endure, a path of survival.

PART FOUR

TRIALS

13

First Meeting

February 2012

I drive to the Golden Cross nursing home. It's in West Fresno, populated by mostly Latinos and African Americans. It's the poor side of town, across the tracks, low income, older homes, few businesses. Japanese Americans once dominated this area, the Buddhist temple was there, along with the Japanese Christian churches. My wife and kids used to go to church in this area; they often drove close to the Golden Cross facility for years on their way to church events and activities.

As I drive, I think of the mausoleum for Japanese Americans where our family made an annual visit at Memorial Day. The names of the Sugimoto clan were present, including those of two infants who died. But there was no plaque for Shizuko. The family did acknowledge her existence: family trees included her name. The children were ranked by age and Shizuko was the fourth of nine children, the eldest daughter. But her death was left open, even though we assumed she had passed: she lacked a symbol of closure and was left in a state of eternal limbo, her soul destined to wander.

The facility is crowded. For the first-time visitor, you immediately feel uncomfortable. The faint but distinct smell of urine. The odd cries and noises emanating from inside rooms. Patients strolling in the hallways, limping, in walkers, in wheelchairs. A woman shrieks in one room, a piercing wail that sends shivers down my spine. I can't help but turn my head to peek in. No one responds to the cry for help because this is nothing out of the ordinary. Then the cries stop, and the woman returns to shaking her head. It's all typical. I'm the outsider.

One older man reaches for my arm, wants me to stop, but I'm unsure of what he wants. In another room a man grumbles to himself, tosses and turns in bed, then his mouth opens and closes, lips move but no words are spoken. A staff person gently talks to the man, subtly provides a pat on his shoulder to skillfully calm him down. It works.

Not many visitors in this facility. You sense they are filled to capacity. This may be the last hope for the residents; they are alone, sick and ill, most old, some with a physical disability, a few others with mental health issues and disorders. Forgotten. All are hidden away from the world, behind convenient walls so I am shielded from them. Until now.

I see the name outside her doorway: Shizuko Sugimoto. I have the right room.

Shizuko rests in the bed, body curled and alone. Her face is calm. Her shiny white hair frames her face. A roommate whines and cries out loud, sending a chill across my skin. Shizuko lies still, sick to death with this long journey.

She is dying; a stroke knocked her off her feet and displaced her balance. Her wheelchair sits to the side, her typically paddling feet silent, empty tennis shoes stacked in the closet. She does not look familiar. I do not see a "Sugimoto" trait other than that she is tiny and Asian. The bed and blankets become her shroud, protecting her and eclipsing her body. A lone note taped to the wall near her bed simply reads "Sugi." I discover our lost aunt.

A family's reunion with history and the abandoned enigma that can no longer be denied. Spirits of the past return and are alive. I should wait to explore family mysteries until all have passed away and only the ghosts remain. Yet Shizuko lives. A curious drive compels me to approach the inner cave of unknowns.

How do you tell your family that after seventy years, you "found" their sister and aunt? None of us had not seen her since 1942. No one knew anything about her. There are no photographs of her existence, no evidence of another child, sister, aunt. We may vaguely recall someone casually mentioning there was "this other" sibling, but that was all.

How will your family respond? I have no fantasy with dramatic documentary close ups of an emotional family reunification. I do not imagine powerful musical crescendos to bridge the decades of separation and flashbacks of a poor immigrant family reliving a nightmare. I do not envision scripted narratives reflecting the stark impact of an epic described in a cracking voice. Instead, I'll respond honestly and authentically.

Confusion. Disbelief. Mixed emotions. Pain. Sorrow. Shame. Muted joy. And at the same time, Shizuko is dying.

All this challenges my peaceful life. I'm forced to step into a dark history, descend into a black hole of family enigmas. I'm not supposed to know all this. I don't want to know. Easier to run and hide, pretend this doesn't exist. Why disrupt all my family had worked so hard to overcome? No shame in being invisible; you can't see your reflection. Yet I'm compelled and pulled into a family epic. Each piece of information reveals a complex narrative, every account helps take away another piece of pain. I recall a simple Buddhist lesson—"Things that cannot be hidden: the sun, the moon, the truth."

Family mysteries haunt us all. No one has a perfect past. Those who believe they do are fools. They ignore stories. Race has always played a role. Religion both unites and divides us throughout time. There will always be the poor and the disadvantaged, the injured and the disenfranchised who are often wrongly forced to live in a separate and challenging universe. Our past defines us, and we live with the ghosts that bind us.

Some stories remain private, concealed, hidden beneath the ground, out of sight and clandestine. Do I disrespect my family's ancestors and keep secrets secret? They had worked hard, so hard, to establish themselves and scratch out a new reality in a world that had imprisoned them. They sought closure on a terrible past, straining to move on, to carve a new history and reconciliation. I open and expose old wounds. I disrupt the journey, face inner demons, and revisit a painful moment no one has asked to return to.

If the family reunites with Shizuko, it would be the first time since the 1940s. For my mom, it would be the first time since that August day in 1942 when the sheriff came to take Shizuko away, a few days before the entire family would be rounded up and imprisoned. Seventy years. Seven decades of separation. A lifetime of struggle and change. For all parties, much had been experienced, forgotten, lost, and now found.

I am struck by her size, small and compact, folded in a fetal position. She appears comfortable, breathing gently, as if asleep. She lays motionless and alone, real and authentic. This is not historical research conducted safely behind words, photographs, and artifacts. I touch her warm hand, feel a bony shoulder, hear a soft sigh as she moves her head to one side. She embodies all that is wrong and right in the world, the sorrow and joy of life, the guilt and happiness of family. She delivers light to our dark past: she complicates and completes us. The family saga continues.

To forge forward
means to forget
without denial.

14

No Place to Go

How does Shizuko measure time? Infants have a very limited sense of time; toddlers up to about the age of four or five understand basic concepts like before and after. Shizuko, as a child, knows how time passes, when her family left for field work, the gap between a breakfast and lunch. Perhaps she grasped the difference between something that took a long time versus a short time. Typically, children first are exposed to structured time when they start school, but Shizuko never attended school.

If she had aged a few more years before the disease impacted her, she would have a different sense of time. She could have understood how long things take or how to read a clock, and the function of counting and attaching words to time. Instead, I imagine she simply lives day to day, unaware of the passing

days, months, and years. Every day she returns to the same place and time, which may be a blessing comfort or a tragic time-loop purgatory repeating over and over. Perhaps this is how she survived, separated from her family, housed in institutions, hidden from the public. Shizuko learns the magic of how to blur the past with the future and masters how to live in the now.

But how does she see herself? Her imagination allows her to expand her view and behavior. She acts out, expresses her dislike for something by throwing it.

"Feisty" describes her from family stories.

And what does she see in the mirror? Someone pretty? Someone strong? Can she make it in this world? Perhaps not as a misfit or outcast but as a innovator. Like blue eyes. We all start with brown eyes, but for some, DNA alters the pigment in some infants' eyes, the brown mutates to blue, a mutation often perceived in America as positive, not as a defect.

Shizuko.

She looks in the mirror.

She sees blue eyes.

I sit down with my mom. I call my aunt and ask her to have a seat. I have news.

"Remember your sister, Shizuko?" I say.

"Of course we remember."

"Oh, she passed a long, long time ago."

"Why?"

I then say: "I got a phone call. I went to see her." Pause. "I wanted to verify." Breathe. "Check firsthand . . ." Delay. "Aunt Shizuko is alive. She's living in Fresno."

A gasp. Silence. Then disbelief.

"What?"

"How can it be?"

"We thought . . . after all those years . . ."

"Oh my god."

I try to explain. My descriptions are sketchy. I don't know all the details.

I'm unsure of all the facts. I share the story of the census and the Wildrose Funeral home. It's confusing and disjointed. I share a description of my initial visit with Shizuko.

Hesitation in voices.

"No. It can't be . . ."

"Who told you all this?"

"How did you find out?"

"I'm confused . . . thought she had died . . ."

An uneven conversation follows. Sentence fragments. Phrases incomplete. Hushed voices. Quiet. The unspoken. Eyes blink from disbelief, then they dart back and forth. Thoughts spin out of control. Lips tighten. Trying to make sense of it all. A silence, then bursts of emotion.

"I can't believe it . . . I can't believe it."

"It can't be."

"I don't believe it . . ."

More questions and I try to answer them.

"Are you sure?"

"But no one survives all those years alone, do they?"

"How did she end up back in Fresno?"

"What does she look like?"

Pauses. Mixed silence and disbelief.

"Visit who? Wait . . . I need to think . . ."

"We all thought she was gone."

"See her? I need time . . . that would upset me too much . . ."

"Where is she?"

"How is she?"

Gradually, recognition and reflection settles in

"Will she recognize us?"

"A stroke? How bad? Is she in pain?"

"Will she know us?"

"We all thought she was gone."

"When can we see her?"

It's about survival. Life like a Greek tragedy, acts unfold as actors play out day to day scenes at the mercy of gods. Life in a time loop. We struggle, we are challenged, we respond, if fortunate, with resilience. Then it repeats. You can't escape the past; it returns to haunt and live with you. Emotions churn unresolved. Anger. Shame. Acceptance. Frustration. Tolerance. We are both driven and oppressed, industrious and inferior. The cycle continues. It's life.

I escaped much of the trauma of immigration, of racism, of poverty. Yet now Shizuko's presence triggers a sense of history I cannot escape. Nor do I want to. I feel someone must pay for the struggles of the past—but what would be justice? I'm reminded that context matters: life was different then, context helps place perceptions and judgments. But does that make a difference today and justify actions and reactions?

Who am I and how does Shizuko make me different? Can I make it in the world like my family, like Shizuko? I don't know. No one knows. I'm isolated yet part of something greater than the self. To suffer and live, the timeless quest.

Japanese Americans endured prison during World War II. My family was one of the last to leave Gila River Relocation Center. When questioned where to assign the train ticket, they chose Fowler, California. Not because they had a farm to return to nor a home they owned and the roomfuls of their personal property that were safely stored. They simply had no other place to go. When dreams were slaughtered, the family had scattered.

When they came home, familiar spring breezes offered a breath of fresh air, yet the ghosts of the recent past lingered. My family returned to the fields that were desperate for laborers. A postwar economy was beginning to flourish, and Americans hungered for real food and quickly discarded the ration books that restricted the purchase of certain foods due to shortages and the need to feed soldiers overseas. Once again, my family of immigrants and misfits helped to feed a nation.

Like the thousands of Japanese Americans, they found their way back to the land they call home—not Japan but America. They trickled back to the West Coast, desperately trying to rebuild their lives; they felt ungrounded and displaced. Some found sanctuary in cities. Many returned to the rich farmlands of the San Joaquin Valley in California, seeking opportunities and the potential for new work in the fields. Opportunities grew in the warmth of spring—life flourished for the Nisei as the Issei aged.

The war lingered for many. Families were refused service at restaurants and hotels. Some businesses posted signs that read: "We don't want any JAPS back here . . . ever!" Military veterans and their families still saw the Japanese Americans as their enemy. Nisei farmers often could not buy farm supplies required for spring work. Vendors refused to sell to them shears, clippers, shovels, and even simple knives. Some Nisei turned inwards and banded together to form their own self-reliant farmers' cooperatives in order to combat the hostile world they faced. These farmers did business with trusted partners. The journey of their peaches and nectarines followed a rigid path: they were first grown by Japanese Americans, then trucked by Japanese Americans, and finally, distributed by Japanese Americans. They survived by becoming invisible, their reward for surviving. By the end of this food chain, these fruits bore their hidden fingerprints that consumers could not see.

Quietly and stealthy, the Nisei rebuilt lives surrounded by fear and hate. They chased the American Dream by believing in the ethos of hard work, trusting one day their labors will be recognized. They could imagine a future.

My mom quietly whispered a story, rarely shared, from her own point of view. When the family returned, they missed their late father's Japanese garden and his handcrafted temples and pagodas. My mom said "she" had taken some of them. "She" was the sheriff's wife who fancied the wooden artwork. Were they gifts to the sheriff to take care of Shizuko? A bribe? Or did "she" simply lay claim to the property like stolen artwork during a war?

"I can't see her.
After all the years
It would be too hard.
Too hard."

15

The Secret of Silence—Letting Go

Another twist. I do not know and will never know how Shizuko navigates those years in confinement. I wish there was a hidden camera to document her drive, her acts of survival, her internal vigor and energy. I do know she emerges decades later with attitude. She stands out. I uncover stories of her wandering from room to room, making her own way in a continuous journey. I imagine her being stubborn, utilizing her tiny frame to impose a cloak of innocence. She understands the discordant hum of human voices and works them to her advantage. She gets help to survive, this we know. She draws attention.

She faces daily tests and a succession of trials. She turns inward, finds something to help her endure, accepts who she is and isn't. Later, she acts out, I understand, manifesting quirky behavior like quietly poking others with her finger and teasing staff. They call her "feisty." Her presence as her witness. Grit. Her own mentor. She processes shame and translates it into survival. She manages to be OK without humiliation and remorse.

A rumor. A story. A riddle. During a childhood naming game while growing up, one cousin casually mentioned we had a lost aunt. The older cousins knew both sides of our family and quizzed us: "How many aunts do you have?"

I'd stop and recite seven names out loud.

My cousins would tease, "But you forgot your mom, she's my aunt too. That's eight!"

Then an older cousin then quipped, "Nine!"

We all stopped and used our fingers to count. A few of us knew about the very short marriage and the first wife of an uncle.

As we nodded our heads, one more cousin announced, "Ten."

We challenged that number, and a trump card was played.

"Akiko." We were reminded of the brass name plate at the cemetery mausoleum.

"She died as an infant but was still family."

Then later, another story was circulated.

Innuendos haunted the cousins. It was casually mentioned at a gathering, spoken in a low tone as if a deep, dark curse was shared between us kids. "There was one more, an aunt. . . . " It was then rudely whispered, " . . . retarded."

The tale was never confirmed nor verified but it stayed with me, teasing and bedeviling my thoughts of family.

The family members involved have died. Years ago, at the funeral of one uncle, the story was rekindled when one cousin casually mentioned that her father was the last to see Shizuko. My curiosity stirred. I learned of a possible secret: my grandmother and this one uncle supposedly had visited Shizuko after the war while she still lived in the area.

I try to reimagine the details as a series of snapshots. A shutter *click, click, click* of personal histories. Visual clues that capture a broader story and narrative. Shizuko was housed at various small institutions for persons with mental health conditions and physical disabilities. She was always on the move, adjusting and starting over and over. Our family had just returned from four years of imprisonment. They were trying to reestablish a home in a land that hated them. A few good neighbors lent a hand, but the family also faced soldiers who were returning from the Pacific front and were still fighting "an enemy." The public distrusted the "Japs." My mom recalls a trip to Sacramento with one of her brothers. They had to map out their drive because gas stations and restaurants were closed to them. They heard the phrase, "We don't serve your kind here." They had to make up their own Japanese American version of *The Green Book*, a publication for African Americans traveling initially in the South but later across our nation. This publication listed safe places where Black people would be welcomed and could eat, get gas, and find lodging. Avoiding confrontation, my family chose to be unseen, a survival technique.

From what I can piece together, as the Sugimoto family tried to rebuild their lives in the Fresno area after internment, Baachan Sugimoto initiated a search for Shizuko with one of her sons. It took years to locate her and arrange a visit, even though the family had little or nothing to offer. They were still struggling for the basics of food and shelter, picking up odd farm work where they could, desperately trying to reconstruct a life that had been ruptured.

Uncertain of what they'd discover, a mother and son journeyed to a distant facility, reportedly in Porterville, California. Shizuko had indeed survived. Did they recognize each other after years of painful separation? Did they relive the tearing departure? Did they hug and cry, sit and talk? Or had the years of separation created gaps and distance? Perhaps to Shizuko these faces were strangers from a foggy memory.

The rumor I heard was that they found that Shizuko was doing OK, better than they could provide as a poor farmworker family. They opted to leave her institutionalized because they had no means to take care of one more person, especially someone with special needs. They felt inadequate and incompetent. They had failed. They once again understood shame. Shizuko had persevered and seemed to carve an identity for herself within the black hole of institutional care of the past.

My grandmother and uncle vowed to never speak of that visit, let the past remain in the past. Was that wrong? This is family. This is us. My grandmother understood the greater love for her daughter was to let go.

Japanese Buddhists believe that after someone dies, their apparition remains for a while in limbo, not earthbound but not yet reborn in the pure land. This is especially true if there was unfinished business here on earth or family members were not well and were left behind suffering.

One term in Japanese is *ganbatteru*, which means "I'm OK." It literally translates into "do your best."

It can be used to tell someone: "I'm OK, so you don't need to worry about me." I've heard stories of Japanese going to the *ohaka*, or "gravesite," of a loved one and talking to the dead. They'd say *ganbatteru* to the deceased, trying to convince them to stop worrying and, in turn, freeing them from familial obligations to bear and endure the burdens of suffering. Only then could the dead move on.

I believe Baachan Sugimoto said that to Shizuko at the end of this one and only visit. In an odd twist of fate, Shizuko seemed better off than the family. Baachan Sugimoto freed her daughter by letting her know that the family was all ok. "*Ganbatteru.*"

No one shared whether or not Shizuko recognized them, a missing final photograph of farewell.

Accept fate and let go
by not remembering.

16

The Great Escape

Shizuko is transferred one more time. She leaves the Fresno area and the smaller facilities that housed her and enters a massive institution in the foothills east of Sacramento, tucked away in the Sierra Nevada. Another test. Another ritual of trials. Away from home. But no matter; she has learned to take home with her and survive. The outstretched arm that catches her is her own.

Initiation and transformation. Shizuko wrestles with the spirits and the power to define herself—by herself.

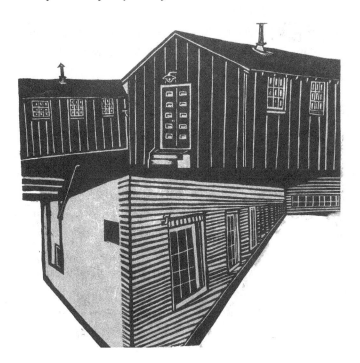

DeWitt State Hospital was originally a military hospital built in 1944 with the expectation there would be massive casualties from the war in the Pacific. In 1947, the facility was redesignated as a psychiatric hospital and gradually re-equipped to receive people with mental health issues. In California during the 1950s, patients were transferred to larger institutions such as DeWitt—which reached a capacity of over 2,800 by 1960. Because of confidentiality, we have no record of when Shizuko first was admitted. We do know she called this home until the early 1970s.

In 1945 and 1946, the relocation camps that imprisoned Japanese Americans were shuttered. The Sugimoto family had begun to disperse, a prelude to the American family diaspora; some aunts and uncles moved to Los Angeles while others returned to farms in the Fresno area where they could find work as farmworkers. By the 1950s, both sides of my family, the Masumotos and the Sugimotos, had purchased farms or were in the early stages of buying farmland. Finally, they were achieving the American immigrant dream: purchasing property, establishing homes and families.

They quietly planted roots in a foreign soil. To escape the past in order to be accepted by buying a piece of America. This is how it works: remuneration and ownership of identity.

I journeyed to the DeWitt Hospital grounds in 2015 to explore and search for clues about Shizuko's life. DeWitt had long ago ceased to be hospital or a psychiatric institution. Sutter County had assumed ownership of the sprawling 200-acre facility. Some buildings were converted to a senior center while others served as county offices. The historical society was housed there. As I drove up the foothills of the Sierras, the scenery unfolds in spectacular colors of green. A crisp spring day, blue skies with a slight fresh breeze. I turn a bend and a small town appeared, along with a sprawling facility.

The layout was intact. Long barracks, formerly living quarters, were connected by perpendicular hallways that ran along one end as an aisle for staff. The buildings were designed with long passageways and the rows and rows of windows perfectly spaced along each wall. At first, I didn't notice, but later realized there were very few doors in proportion to the number of barracks. Because all the rows and rows of windows were elevated high off the ground, no one could climb in or out without injury.

I peeked inside a few of the structures and found long rooms with fading linoleum flooring, gray today but perhaps once a brighter color. One building was number 320A. Was that the total number of structures at this site? Possibly, because there was a legion of small bungalow homes for the nursing, medical, and educational workers who lived on site.

Some halls still had a large swamp cooler attached to one end of the barrack atop a wooden stand. Swamp coolers are designed with a huge fan housed in a large metal box with a vented opening that channeled air into a strong stream. The sides were covered with pads that absorbed water dripping from hoses to cool the air. I can imagine dry, hot summers with a fan blowing air into the interiors, a minor cooling derived from the mist on three sides of the cooler. This basic system typically worked in many old farmhouses: it added humidity to the air, a refreshing respite from the dreadful heat. I grew up with swamp coolers. Our present-day old farmhouse still employs this technology, a simple and adequate connection with the past and nature. Our valley has dry intense heat and I have learned to live with it and not control it. I can picture Shizuko standing in front of the blowing fan, the moist and slightly cooler air streaming over her face, her hair flutters, her loose clothes flap and for a moment she's transported.

I read that briefly, during World War II, German prisoners of war were housed at the DeWitt site. In addition, the original design anticipated a long, drawn out battle in the Pacific and the countless wounded soldiers who would need to be housed in long-term recovery units here. But the war ended abruptly with the bombing of Hiroshima and Nagasaki and the Army never required the spacious grounds. I thought about this as I trudged through the grounds, accompanied by the twisted fact that the Sugimoto family was originally from Hiroshima. My mom and her family had cousins impacted by the bomb. We lost most contact with that side of the family. Along with, of course, Shizuko.

I wandered where Shizuko once wandered. I stood under shade trees where I imagined she once rested. I peeked into the same cafeteria and the boarded-up gym where she would have spent time. I felt the spirits of the thousands housed, incarcerated, imprisoned here. They too walked these grounds, vanquished in their random, roaming thoughts.

I can recall this sensation. I felt the same chill in the air in 1979 when I first visited Gila River Relocation Center in Arizona, home to my family during World War II. I shuffled through the barren landscape, the open grid pattern of streets and blocks still etched into the earth, cement blocks and foundations telltale markers of a desert city of 10,000 internees. As I slept in the back of my pickup truck, a frigid wind blew throughout the night. I could feel the voices of thousands of spirits left behind, trying to make sense of their history. I felt despair: there was no future here.

The ghosts remain bound to a place. Ties that bind me to a history.

Like Gila River, the ghosts of DeWitt Hospital were quiet. They spoke few words. The silence piercing. You can't escape the history here.

But I tried. Unlike the relocation camps of World War II, today in 2015 there was life at DeWitt Center. One building on the edge housed a WIC program, a government-funded program to provide assistance to women and children, often through food vouchers. A health clinic created activity in another structure. A senior center brought an older community onto the grounds, possibly for a Meals on Wheels noontime lunch program.

I talked with some seniors at the historical society office and library. One had worked at DeWitt. She paused but the years had passed and names and faces blurred. I wondered if she could have known Shizuko. Another was the music teacher with many stories of her years working with the vast array of patients. But no closure. No discovery of a story that could fill in the blanks. Ghosts don't leave behind records.

Destiny to leave unresolved. Fated to remain unsettled. I had built my own private prison of the undefined: to catch, tame, and tolerate the apparitions.

While some of the Sugimoto family found some success in reestablishing themselves with a farm of their own, Shizuko had descended into a deeper dark cavern of a huge, impersonal institution. Yet she survived. Unable to escape her past, perhaps she forged a path to try.

Succumb to the past in order to live in the future.

17

Blue Moon

"Blue Moon"

    A slow, pensive song popularized in the 1930s and later in 1949 by the deep and gentle voice of Billy Eckstine.

    A blue moon is the second full moon in a single month. A rare occurrence. A chance viewing. A stroke of luck.

I interview a retired music teacher who taught at DeWitt State Hospital for decades in the 1950s and '60s. She has no specific recollection of

Shizuko but refers to the multitude of "her" students. She shares stories of working with mental patients, bringing music in many forms to their lives. They formed percussion bands, banging on drums, tapping wood blocks, a few blowing on whistles and song flutes. I picture Shizuko joining the gang, beating out her own rhythm, joyfully pounding with a stick, swinging a bell and shaking a rattle. The clamor was wild, intense, and completely free.

Initially I feel sorry for the music teacher as her students belted out a rhythm, hammering an inconsistent beat, thrashing their instruments with erratic and capricious intensity, and never keeping time in a linear and orderly fashion. I suggest that it must have sounded chaotic, unruly, and disruptive.

But she corrects me: "It was music to my ears."

I try to imagine Shizuko making music with this gentle and understanding teacher. Not as a fabrication but something that "could have been"—a touchstone to a moment I can keep. Now I have sounds to accompany my memories. I had believed only factual accounts made for real history. The lack of physical artifacts had restricted my sense of the past. But Shizuko is not on trial. Creating memory is not about weighing what was verified and right versus something felt and thus wrong. Conjecture: the freedom to explore and imagine.

The music teacher then shared details of the hospital campus's big band she helped to organize. At first, I believe it was composed of the patients, but she said, "No, it was made up of staff who played at a monthly dance for the rest of the personnel." Held in the wood floor gym, their Saturday night or special holiday dances attracted hundreds of employees, all dressed in party clothes. Occasionally, clusters of patients crowded around the open double doors, straining to get a peek inside and watch the couples floating across the dance floor, swinging and whirling to the sound of the big band. One very popular slow dance song they played was "Blue Moon."

I recall a conversation with my mom about music and her teen years while confined in the relocation camps. They listened to songs. They held high school dances where they swayed to the sounds from records. Later they formed their own big band sounds from a collection of musicians composed of fellow inmates with saxophones, trumpets, and singing voices.

They were kids, growing up behind barbed wire, trying to make the most of a terrible situation. The music helped distract, pass the time, cope. For a few brief minutes, they could imagine a different place and time in the future. "Of course, we listened to upbeat songs, like 'Keep Your Sunnyside Up,'" my mom shared. "But we also liked the slow dance songs, including 'Blue Moon,'" she giggled.

"Blue Moon." With lyrics that depicted someone standing alone and feeling blue, without dreams and without love. But then, someone suddenly appears with an adoring whisper and the moon turns to gold.

This bittersweet song captured the spirit of my mother and many Japanese Americans. Their dreams crumbled, their lives robbed of love and affection. Yet they clung to an optimism that some good would happen. Perhaps only "once in a blue moon"—an idiom which implies something rarely occurs—their fantasy of freedom and a normal life could, would, and should happen eventually. A song with the sound of hope with time.

> Otsukimi—*moon viewing. In Japan, an annual autumn festival celebrating the full moon with food and music as villagers gather in hope of a bountiful harvest. The bright glow in the night sky symbolizes abundance and the anticipation of good fortune, recognizing the beauty that honors life.*

The moon changes every month, and our Gregorian calendar system does not match the shifts. A lunar month fits a cycle of approximately twenty-seven to twenty-eight days. A blue moon favors us only once every two or three years and signifies a special instance to pause and acknowledge.

On our farm, I have my own moon viewing traditions while working at night. Once my eyes adjust to the dark, I'm amazed by the brightness of a full moon. I discover I can do much without the sun or artificial light.

In the darkness, a realization impacts me: I am not alone. I first think of the select group of others who also labor in the night during the graveyard shift. Déjà vu then sweeps over me. I reunite with ghosts who have also performed night chores on this piece of land. We trudge through the fields together, marching to a different beat, heeding a unique calling.

I think of my father as a young man, struggling to make a go of it on our farm, saving money by doing most of the work himself. This meant laboring late into the night, especially when he worked a separate day job on another farm, only to come home and start his second job on his own land in the evening and eventually with the stars. I think of my grandparents hustling, performing tasks that were often paid by piece work—the more vines they pruned or raisins they picked, the more money they earned. Long after the sun had set, the waning light provided opportunity and hope.

I've often irrigated the orchards and vines in the dark as a night irrigator. I'd have only a few hours to push the water down a row. I slip into repetitive tasks, shoveling dirt, connecting water at the ends of rows, offering a drink to thirsty trees. In the darkness I can hear the flow of the water streaming out of the cement valves to judge the volume and force. I can see the reflection of the moon on the water in the furrows to determine how far it had traveled. My senses adjust to the natural light of the moon.

My night work is unscheduled and inconsistent, often resulting from a weather crisis or equipment failure. A full moon delivers a chance to grow life on a farm.

A curious nature about work at night: I feel like it's untimed. Clocks seem to stop. Unlike the daylight when I can estimate the time of day by simply looking up and measuring the position of the sun, using the moon to measure time is complicated. An overhead moon does not equate with midnight; a moon on the horizon does not necessarily indicate a specific time. I lack the other typical indicators like meals or break times that divide the shift.

During a moonlit night I find myself walking alone. I lose myself in thoughts shrouded in darkness. I hum a song of night work—routine noise echoes differently, sounds carry a different significance. I can hear distinctly the dirt crunching beneath my boots, the shovel slicing into the earth, the irrigation water trickling then splashing into a furrow—a harmony fills the still air. A slower cadence matches my pace as I lumber from one irrigation valve to the next, adjusting the flow of water by the sound as it spills out. No rush as I have all night. I trust my judgment from years of experience and know the water will reach the end of the row by morning. Calm. Repose. Tranquil. Working alone, happy alone.

Then a gentle melody floats above me, hovers at the treetops before rising into the night air. A song is altered with the night air. The exact lyrics or melody do not matter as I slip into a trance with a different spirit: a freedom to ponder.

I recall the story of the DeWitt music teacher talking of her decades of work when Shizuko too resided at the facility. I can hear the music of the monthly dances.

Late October 1955 at DeWitt State Hospital

The music escapes from the gym doors into the warm summer night air. I imagine Shizuko taking advantage of her tiny body to squeeze in-between others to get a front row peek into the magical gym filled with couples effortlessly gliding across the floor. After a few minutes, as the melody and lyrics drift overhead, she slips back, away from the doors, and stands alone in the open ground. She looks up at the full moon. The bright glow gently illuminates her face as she peers upwards, a sheen casts across her gentle face, a momentary calm connection. Blue moon, a rare second full moon that lazy October evening.

Music ignites the power to imagine. With sensory stimulation I reimagine and feel. Shizuko and the music of a night, the sounds and imagery make her story visceral. Because it's abstract, I'm allowed to feel. Shining more light on Shizuko does little good since there's so little known about her. But in the shadowy moonlight Shizuko comes to life. I can personify history. In the night, my imagination allows me to touch Shizuko and she touches me. I sever my old sense of what was real in order to open myself to something new.

Late October 1955 at the Sugimoto family farm

In September and October, our family made raisins by picking green grapes, first placing them on paper trays (the industry had modernized, shifting from bulky wooden trays to paper) lying on the ground in between vine rows and then witnessing the sun drying them into dark, caramel treats over the course of weeks. Thousands of trays required constant monitoring. Only with intensive hand labor could the harvest be completed.

After curing, every tray needed to be rolled into a biscuit-like spiral shape and then collected from the fields. With an autumn heat wave, raisins can begin to overdry, and dreams could wither in the harsh sunlight. As a result, often the family marched back out to complete the back breaking "rolling" in the evening to avoid the extreme one-hundred-degree heat of daytime. In tough financial years, the family hustled to work a full day at other farms then at night they tend to their own crop and their own harvest.

On a full moon night, Baachan Sugimoto returned to the family farm to help with raisins. She toiled with her sons, crawling from tray to tray, bundling another batch of raisins, one final step in a long year of growing and now harvesting. The sound of the crumpling paper could be heard in the adjacent rows as the family labored down one row and then another. At the end of one row, Baachan stopped and paused, stood up and stretched momentarily, arms behind her, pushing against lower back muscles. She looked up at the moon illuminating the night sky.

For a moment, they shared the same blue moon—mother and daughter, parent who had lost a child and the lost child. Reunited not in person but with a shared reflection, the moon bridging the distance. They accepted the fact that they would never be together but that never stopped their desire or devotion. They could long for a shared emotion, like a wish but not a dream because they knew it would never happen. They accepted the separation that defined their lives. And then they moved onward, without guilt or remorse; the pendulum continuing to swing, another row, another day.

I want to believe this happened. Not as a false association when the brain reinforces fabrications and can no longer distinguish the unfounded from the real. Not part of a theory of confirmation bias when eyewitness accounts become unreliable. This story embodies an emotional legacy, building empathy through imagination in order to accept Shizuko into our family. I restore memory by creating memory and reclaiming the past. My aim is to help clarify and justify a commitment to the present.

I do not have detailed records, yet that does not imply experiences have vanished, never to be found. If our family had wealth, we'd have photographs. The powerful could pay for documentation to verify their own histories. I move beyond constraints of now and break through the perceived boundaries of experience based on privilege. No one recorded my family's journey. I have only a few relics from before the war to validate their experiences. Stories were not passed down helping me to recollect—until now when I can time travel in order to understand.

How can I remember when there is so little to remember? In the world of disabilities, individuals were wrongly sheltered and cast away, hidden and invisible. The images of the everyday were rarely documented, yet these moments tell me the real story.

My limited perspective isolated me from my family. I struggled by seeking information instead of sensations. I looked backwards, collecting the details anchored by dates and places. I rarely employed emotions and feelings. For example, according to passports I discovered, Jiichan Masumoto arrived in America in 1897, Baachan Masumoto in 1918. There, I have history . . . or not, because what does a date tell me? Then I discovered the telegram my Baachan Masumoto sent from the ship *Kashima Maru*, sailing from Japan to America where she was to meet my grandfather. July 2, 1918—the telegram read: "Arrive Seattle Wednesday." The abruptness sheds light on that passage because my grandfather at that time was working on a farm in Sanger (outside of Fresno, California), a thousand miles from Seattle. There's no reference to which Wednesday, and it ignores the fact that immigrants were forced to endure days and weeks in quarantine. The resulting confusion tells me more about legacy than any date and place.

I now can see Shizuko as treasured inheritance. I envision her in an abstract series of snapshots and sounds woven together when checkable facts are absent. I can make notes of little things—like the story of a frantic out-of-rhythm beat and the kindness of a music teacher. Shizuko is accepted as she is.

My path to remember lies in triggering the senses: the music and sounds of real life; the ability to see clearer in the shadows where my family lived; the tactile world of night work that opens windows into experience and connections. Days gone by come alive and have meaning in the present.

My family did not listen to music, but I grew up with a language of time surrounding me.

Japanese was spoken in our home, yet I never mastered the language. I then moved and lived in Japan for almost two years, blending the modern Japanese language with the rural dialect of my family—*Kumamoto-ben*. In addition, much of the pidgin Japanese in our home originated in the Japan of the late 1800s and later became fused with words borrowed from English. My speech was forever twisted, a fusion of two worlds, a misfit tongue.

One of my challenges was with the subjunctive mood or causal inference, especially with verb tense and the premise that the way we talk helps to determine the way we see the world.

In English, we identify time with indicators: the past, present, and future tense, all identified with key terms or spelling. We ran. We run. We will run.

In Japanese, there is a past tense signifying something that happened before: *ikimashita*, or "I went." But the terms for "I go" or "I will go" are the same—*ikimasu*. You can only determine the present versus the future tense by context, what the speaker or writer implies. "I go now" versus "I will go tomorrow"—*ima*, or "now," *ikimasu*. *Ashita*, or "tomorrow," *ikimasu*.

One theory is that Japanese see the future in the present. The two time dimensions are blurred together, without a clear division. An economist claims that's why Japanese—and other Asian countries with a similar language syntax—often save much more money than other countries. The theory is founded on the belief that Japanese think of the future in the present, there's no separation of the two, both can be felt simultaneously.

The syntax of Japanese filled our home; it was my music of family. Embedded in not only the words but also the implicit meaning. In my quest to find Shizuko I discover a twist in meaning of language. As a child, her spoken language was limited. In our first meeting no words were exchanged. Yet the weight of culture hangs over us: words do not fully explain, feelings belong in our expanding story and congeal into the fabric that connects us. We will learn to make our own music.

To live in the moment. To witness the beauty and radiance of a full moon. To accept the eternal loneliness of separation. Witness the past in the present. Buddhist suffering as hope. And then destiny to move on.

Yet I continue to struggle with my family's meaning, wrestling with culpability, grappling with responsibility, feeling remorse then guilt for trying to make sense of this saga. I wish things had been different but hurt with the reality of what happened. I live with generational trauma, inherited regret and shame. I am unsure how I would have survived and coped. Will I ever grasp the meaning to persevere? My initiation remains incomplete; I cannot see the future in the present.

To reimagine and construct new memories empowers me to forge relationships. Like a eulogy at a funeral, the stories embody the life and meaning of the dead. We don't fact check eulogies for verifiable accuracy. We accept them for what they are: ingredients of the memory we want to take with us. Life captured as a legend in lieu of written documentation. In the Western world, we cast doubt on oral traditions, empowering authorities to write trusted accounts. Yet my grandparents were illiterate, so instead, I search for their voices, listening for the songs and whispers of daily life.

I imagine the song "Blue Moon" played under a night sky in October 1955. Shizuko looks up, listens to the music floating up into the night sky. Likewise, Baachan Sugimoto pauses from work and stares at the moon, lost in a trance, lost in time. The music of the night in their souls. Sharing a moment armed with the power of imagination.

For an instant, I disregard the handful of truths I know about Shizuko and allow myself to imagine and fill in gaps. I reach for the fragments of stories and hold them close instead of trying to shed light on them for further study. In the shadows lie the true ghosts of my family. I see more with night vision when

I utilize all my senses. In this murkiness, the obscure takes center stage. I can imagine Shizuko and Baachan Sugimoto sharing a dream.

I will continue to work at night with moonlight as my guide. Occasionally, with luck, I can labor during a blue moon. Magically, a song may also appear as I stand alone in the healing stillness of the fields, surrounded by the power of a farm with footprints of generations and the ties that bind. Seize the moment of connection. I will dream in my heart, hoping stories of my family will appear before me. I can hear voices. Emotions rekindled. Memories adore. No longer alone.

And then the moon will turn to gold.
"Blue Moon"

PART FIVE

WALLS OF SECURITY

18

Family Reunion

My mom visits first. This was the sister she never knew; eight years sepa-rated their ages. When Shizuko contracted meningitis, my mom was not yet born. She never knew this sister and grew up wondering, "What was normal?" As a child, my mom feared Shizuko. "She tossed things and was moody," she explains. So the little sister kept her distance from the older big sister.

Their reunion is muted. Stares trying to take in the moment of disbelief. "This is Shizuko" is repeated as if to help rationalize the situation. Hands reach out and touch. Mom leans over and strokes the face of her sister. Nothing is said. Perhaps because Shizuko is in hospice, the exchange is peaceful. Final closure anticipated, a blessing silence.

The next day, my aunt arrives from Los Angeles to visit. She was closest, two years younger. As soon as she heard about Shizuko, she insisted on rushing to her side. My aunt had distant memories of an active and talk-ative older sister. As the family grew, my aunt would be placed in charge of Shizuko, helping to watch her and take care of the child with "issues."

She goes to the bedside, peers over the resting Shizuko, takes her hands, squeezes tightly, then rubs her arms. She then runs fingers through the sil-very white hair of her dying sister, brushing the delicate hair back in order to uncover and reveal a face.

I sense a rush of emotions—joy, discovery, guilt, shame, confusion. She talks to Shizuko in Japanese, hoping those ancient words might connect and stir memories. Shizuko lies motionless. I feel the heartbeat of the two sisters, the decades of separation erased for a moment.

My aunt witnesses Shizuko stir and believes she recognizes her voice or perhaps the Japanese, the only language Shizuko spoke with family. In a moment of excitement, my cousins also join us in Shizuko's room. Yet nothing. No resolution. As it should be.

My uncle later visits his sister. He too feels the distance and the emotions of unfinished family business. He inquires, "How long will Shizuko live?"

No one quite knows. An African American staff helper comments, "She is one tough lady." We all nod our heads but do not know what that means.

I visit Shizuko over the next few weeks. In my mind, it's somehow fitting that she remains unconscious. I feel a connection with this sedate and subdued body, her history calm, yet an enigma that unites us as she lies in bed, part of hospice. We seek comfort in her last breaths. Natural. Quiet. Touching. I hold her cold hand, squeeze it to try and feel something, anything that might help me know who this lady is and who am I. All we have is touch.

A family gathering, a reunion with the past in the present. It's messy, awkward, and disturbing because of the inherit disconnect. Shizuko wasn't supposed to be here, her odds of survival over the decades was extremely low. No one lives this long institutionalized. Seven decades. Separated and alone. Seventy years. Endures and perseveres.

We family members are not supposed to be reunited with Shizuko. We did not launch a lifelong quest to search for a missing family member. My family understood the traumatic drama of the past they could not control.

Family history does not follow a linear line with a simple beginning, middle and end like a novel or movie. I imagine our past as a series of dots that connect, except that I do not know where the next dot lies despite my best intentions and careful planning. Looking back, the family chronicle swings wildly, the dots never lining up in a linear order and instead zigzagging over time, dictated by powerful forces, people responding as best they could, adapting to nature and human nature. The path twists with the poetic "forks in the road;" however, when you're at one of those forks, you may not even know it. So I stumble with this first family reunion, unsure of myself and a family saga that adds another layer of confusion to our history.

We stand face to face with a secret. I'm a writer but I do not understand this narrative. I cannot conduct an inquiry with the skills of an investigative journalist; my exploration so far has only resulted in incomplete stories. I am embedded in circumstances weighed by a baggage of history with gaps and more gaps. I can't explain this tale with "just the facts" because I don't know all the facts. I actually know very little except that Shizuko lies before me and I find an odd comfort in the silence we share. Her breathing. Turning in bed. Head shifting.

Our family reunion should trigger stories and emotions. Instead, the stillness speaks with clarity: the drama of life overshadows the unknown facts. The meeting exposes the unresolved history that does not yet belong in the present.

I am a Sansei. We are disconnected with older generations. The Issei from Japan typically did not speak English. Few of us learned Japanese. I never had a conversation with either grandmother until I had studied in Japan in my twenties. We Sansei were born "after the camps" and knew little about relocation. I never thought of my parents or grandparents as prisoners of war. We were raised to be American.

Yet I knew I was Japanese. As a kid, I looked in a mirror and wondered how the other kids knew I was Japanese (or most often, they called me "*Chino*," the word for "Chinese" in Spanish). I looked at my reflection and didn't see Japanese . . . but American?

Growing up, I enjoyed watching World War II movies but only the fighting in Europe like *The Longest Day* or *The Dirty Dozen* or *The Great Escape*, and on television we watched *Combat!* and *The Rat Patrol*. I was relieved few movies were about the Pacific front. The only one I watched with intrigue was *Run Silent, Run Deep* because the Japanese were not just the enemy but a respected foe and the story involved more than just external battles; it included themes of vengeance, endurance, courage, loyalty, and honor that were tested during wartime. In a twisted way, it reminded me of how my family survived the war too, except our vengeance was to become more American than Americans.

I am part of a generation imprisoned by our own insecurities: we no longer wear the face of the outsider, the misfit, the enemy. We saved face by not having a face.

For many Issei, relocation and incarceration during World War II destroyed their lives. Grandfather Sugimoto died in camp. Grandfather Masumoto was an old man in his late sixties when they incarcerated him. (In 1940, the life expectancy for men in America was sixty years old.) He knew, for all intents and purposes, his life was over; the government took away all he had.

Nisei endured but had to live with the scars of being prisoners, unwanted and wronged. They stopped dreaming. To live was to simply persevere. The Nisei forged forward, and the next generation arrived. Many families in Central California took huge risks to purchase a family farm in the very country that had imprisoned them. The Nisei recognize they could not change the masks they wore and had to find ways to be accepted. Their mantra: "We will become the quiet Americans."

Sansei like me, inherited this legacy and hid in our own protected world of security. We grew up on family farms without memories of the uprooting and false arrests. Our limited family stories felt right until they weren't. We were sheltered as children, naive and ignorant. Most later escaped the fields and left behind rural roots to find success in the big city and careers far, far from the dirt and sweat of farms. We learned that we could wish for anything.

But our parents and grandparents knew better; lessons of their past never left them. "Don't take chances" was the mantra. We were nudged to pursue safe careers and lives. "Study hard in school. Don't make waves."

We were taught not to question, to move cautiously, not drawing attention and believing in the Japanese proverb *"Deru kui wa utareru,"* or "the nail that sticks out will be hammered down." Conformity is the safe path to becoming American. The family diligently performed the spring ritual of weeding by hand, shovels slicing and purging the unwanted growth. A dance was performed: hands pull weeds, toss them to the side, a shovel for those deep rooted, move to the next and the next, stand to stretch an aching back, repeat.

By all accounts our families were successful, not merely as survivors, but we wore the masks of success: middle-class, land-owning, educated. But at times I fear we lacked significance, rarely occupying power positions, content with a strategy of avoiding failure.

So what's the matter with that?

The staff cares for Shizuko diligently. She responds to them. As family.

A lurking issue hangs over my thinking: who is responsible to take care of family? Who will look after my parents and me as I age? On a family farm, it's traditional that someone stays behind to tend for the family and the land. A son may inherit the farm and unfairly a daughter is often burdened to care for aging parents. Unfair for all because such obligations are not rewarded in our current systems. We don't receive more income because our peaches carry the fingerprints of my father and grandmother.

Ironically, while living and studying in Japan, I visited the village of the Masumotos, the home my grandparents left in the early 1900s. I worked the ancient rice plots of my grandmother's family farm. I lived and slept in the farmhouse she grew up in. Yet while there, I realized rice, even though I had consumed it daily while growing up, was an alien crop to me. I have no history of when to plant it, how to grow it, the means to harvest a livelihood from these grains. That's when I opted to come back to our family farm in California and the familiar scent of a ripening nectarine and the explosive taste in a golden peach. I was pulled back by something: the whisper of voices from the past, the tug from the ghosts of obligation, not in Japan but in America.

Now Shizuko joins this legacy of our family and farm. I feel the familiar sense of unknowns that both plague and yet give life to our organic orchards and vineyards. Failure is part of the world of nature and my work. Mistakes fill my annual ritual of passing seasons. Nothing will ever be perfect and fully understood. The metronome of life continues to pulse; we have our own internal rhythms guiding us. I beat myself over the errors and mistakes but continue to march forward. I walk these fields of gold, listening to the heartbeat of Shizuko.

A reunion of family
and stories.

19

Lost Altars—Our Butsudan

Thus have I heard.

These words begin some of the famous Buddhist scriptures, doctrines supposedly directly from the Buddha and passed down by disciples. These are the "sutras" or teachings to be practiced and shared.

Does Shizuko know she is raised as a Buddhist? Can you be a Buddhist without knowing or acknowledging it? Or because she is Japanese American with a foreign face, will she be judged to be non-Christian, an alien, a non-believer? A Buddhist minister would proclaim that Shizuko's daily life rhythms and suffering make her more Buddhist than any of us typical folk. Thus have I heard.

I visit with the staff at Shizuko's facility. They are kind and gentle and it takes time for them to share stories with me, a stranger. Everyone knows Shizuko. She had been at Golden Cross for about fifteen years, always roaming and wandering the hallways. She was never still and confined to her room; she overcame the walls around her.

They call her "Sugi" and at first, they don't know who I'm talking about when I say "Shizuko" or "Sugimoto." Nicknames are a powerful sign of personal connections. You assign nicknames to people you care about, sometimes in a negative, pejorative demeanor, more often with a positive, affectionate, and cordial tone. "Sugi" I repeat to myself and grin, reminding myself of all the nicknames assigned to me by my elementary school buddies, most who were children of farmworkers. My Spanish nicknames included *"Masa harina,"* or "corn flour," and *"Mas o Menos,"* or "more or less" and a play on my last name. Others blended a fusion of ideas like *"Chapo,"* or "chubby"—think a slightly overweight ten-year-old like myself as a kid and fused with the 1960s pop culture movie and television images of the Asian karate "chop."

The staff are mostly people of color, solid, caring, and few with professional degrees. They have a spirit of compassion, working with the residents with disabilities, alone and often forgotten. Like Sugi was.

The director tells me that Sugi has a home here. She has made a reputation most enjoy. She wants to be seen. She is willing to engage and not accept her limitations. Her disability is not a punishment and not a curse.

I'm comforted by her uncluttered observation. I carry the baggage of an over-simplified Buddhist thought of *karma,* or "cause and effect." Was Shizuko's life story a sequence of cause and effect? Did my family do something bad or wrong and Shizuko bore the consequences? My mind wanders to a broader metaphysical level—was there something in Shizuko's prior life that resulted in the suffering in this life? But I must disable such *karmic* thinking. It's bad *karma.* Thus I have heard.

When our family returned to the Fresno area following their release from the relocation camps, they sought to reclaim some of their belongings. A neighbor—an Armenian—had stored the family *Butsudans,* or "Buddhist altars," hand-crafted by Jiichan Sugimoto before the war. These good neighbors understood persecution when their families had fled the Armenian Genocide in Europe in the early 1900s and sought refuge in America. They sought to survive brutal conditions and massacres in their homeland. Displaced from their villages and farms they came to a country that had often restricted immigration. California became home to thousands, many arriving in the Fresno area to farm the fertile lands, planting roots in the soil here. One nearby settlement was named Yettem, the Armenian word for "Eden." Our family had been introduced to a kind Armenian neighbor; they were willing to store the "pagan" altars of the "enemy" during the war and returned them to my family. And they too were farmers.

Asking for the *Butsudan* took courage. I now see how radical my uncles were, reclaiming who they were and their own march for justice. They did not simply sweep away their past to cleanse themselves. Instead, they directed their emotions to renew their faith in an uncompromising fashion. The artwork of my grandfather, who crafted these *Butsudans*, offered a connective tissue between people and communities, a performance of empathy unfolding between farming communities.

I wonder what their Armenian neighbors thought when initially approached by my family's request before the war. Or perhaps they reached out to my family and explored how they could be of help, recalling their personal possessions they were forced to leave behind. Their own people's history left scars and memories; they understood persecution and a history of intolerance of the faces they wore. They understood the consequences of being different and the power of acknowledging and reclaiming the past as they sought to define what America stood for as a country. They were good neighbors, good farming neighbors.

I grew up with this *Butsudan* in our living room. We'd light candles and make small offerings of white rice at special occasions such as New Year celebrations. Today, our daughter has it in her home, the remodeled farmhouse I grew up in. It now serves another generation.

In our farmhouse we have another *Butsudan*. It's from the Del Rey Buddhist Hall, the temple in the nearby town our family attended for decades. When the community of Japanese American farmers in our area grew old and retired, only a handful of kids took over the farms. With only a few families remaining, we decided to close the temple and sell the property. The *Butsudan*, a handcrafted piece of art sacred to our community, needed a new home. We were one of the only families still working the land and were given the *Butsudan*. It remains safe and secure in our home. We house it in my basement office and as I write, I can occasionally breathe in the scent of incense from the generations of Buddhists.

Thus I have heard.

PART SIX

INITIATION

20

Family Letters

February 4, 2012

Dear Sugimoto Family,

Greetings and a belated Happy New Year. 2012 is the Year of the Dragon and already a rather wild year is unfolding. Some of you may recall that the Sugimoto family had a sister who became separated from the family.

From what I understand, as a child she was severely injured by meningitis, which resulted in significant intellectual disabilities. But she stayed with the Sugimoto family until relocation. She was not allowed to travel to camp and was tragically transferred into state custody.

She has been in state institutions ever since then. Aside from a rumored brief contact following camp, no one was able to keep in touch with her.

A week ago, I received a call. Shizuko Sugimoto, born in 1919, is now in a hospice program at a facility in Fresno. I went to go see her—she is not well. Very, very frail and weak. She is mentally unresponsive but is constantly shifting her body and moving her legs. She is very emaciated. However, she is alive. It was nice to "find" her after all these years.

Since her condition warrants hospice, she will probably not live long. A few days? A few weeks? No one knows for sure. We are in the process of arranging cremation and any end-of-life arrangements.

So I wanted to let everyone know about this "found" aunt and sister!

This is not a call to rush to Fresno (although it would be fun to see relatives!). Shizuko is unresponsive and bedridden.

When she passes, I will try to coordinate some sort of memorial service, probably for an upcoming weekend. Again, this is certainly not to obligate anyone to attend—after all, I'm not sure if any of the cousins ever saw this tiny woman. I will let as many of you as I can know about details. Please share this with all the cousins and family.

It is a wonderful story of lost and now discovered family. A goal is to reunite her with her father and mother and her siblings at the Mountain View Cemetery. A fitting final resting place for a sister, no? She can claim her spot with family.

So be well. We should celebrate this reunion.

Mas

February 17, 2012

Greetings Sugimoto clan!

Visited Aunt Shizuko (still odd to suddenly have a new aunt and a new "auntie name," no?) Another day and no change.

My sense is that she may be in this state for weeks, not just days. But you never know. I did find out that over the past year she has become much, much weaker. A year ago, she sat up daily, sat in her wheelchair regularly. The recent change to her being bedridden prompted the shift to hospice. The staff can stir her enough so she drinks and eats a liquid diet.

Hope that helps!

Mas

March 2012

Sugimoto family,

An update from Fresno and Aunt Shizuko. She remains the same. Unresponsive yet alive. I have no idea how long she will remain in this condition.

There are so many unanswered questions. I visit and she remains alone, lying in bed, still and silent. She looks comfortable and not in pain. But no answers.

I talk with the staff and they relate a few stories. Shizuko was very active. She was in constant motion. Everyone knew her.

We can only learn from these voices but it's hard to put them into the "story of Shizuko." So much more to this soul before me.

We continue to wait.

Thanks.

Mas

April 2012

Family,

I wish I had more to report but there has been no change. Shizuko continues to lie still, as if asleep all the time.

Actually, I suppose no news is good news because she's alive, struggling for life?

Thanks to all who have come for a visit. It was great to see everyone and for a family gathering of sorts. An odd circumstance nonetheless: to connect with a long-lost family member in silence.

But perhaps that's exactly how it should be.

Will keep you posted.

Mas

May 5, 2012

Sugimoto family,

A quick update about Aunt Shizuko: amazingly, she remains the same.

She looks very thin and frail and sleeps all the time. She isn't responsive but every once in a while she opens her eyes. I do not believe she recognizes anything. She quickly closes her eyes and returns to a sleep. She does move around a lot while in bed, as if restless, but I do not believe she's in pain and the staff agrees with such an assessment.

A week ago she did have an incident—becoming very, very agitated and refusing to eat or drink for a day—but she calmed down and returned to her resting state (if that's what you call it).

An update about final plans. I contacted the Fresno Japanese Interfaith Religious Council and after a series of conversations and exchanges, we've made these plans:

Shizuko did not have a "niche" at the Mountain View Mausoleum. This is the mausoleum where the ashes of most of the Sugimoto clan are resting.

I did the paperwork and have purchased a niche for Aunt Shizuko.

There was an open space—it's with Hatsujiro, Masa, Shigeru, and Akiko Sugimoto. The specific space is just below Akiko Sugimoto.

I believe this can reunite Shizuko with her family after all these years.

Again, no change but as you know, at her age anything can happen any day. Frankly, the staff at the home where she has been for the last few years are amazed she is hanging on so well.

Shizuko remains an amazing woman, no?

Thanks.

Mas

21

Photo Identity—Gold Star Mothers

Shizuko wages a private war in order to survive. She had endured decades of her own challenges and struggles. I imagine at times it felt as if in prison, confined in massive state institutions then a series of group homes. She could not have known the saga of her family and the internment camps. But she could share in the emotional pain of being an outcast and castaway in the very contry she claimed as home. And the burden of keeping quiet.

I am the only family member to consistently see Shizuko—the visits feel odd, almost like an exchange with the living dead. But it's not morbid nor melancholy because in a twisted way, I feel as if this is a type of ohaka mairi, meaning "to visit the cemetery and the gravesite of an ancestor." Christians may visit a headstone and feel sorrow and depression with the loss. Many Japanese Buddhists have a different connection with those that have passed before us. Our ancestors watch over and protect the living and they too need our support and care. We pay respect and homage to them, grateful for the path they have created. We need each other.

My impression is that Shizuko was a forgotten misfit, ignored, locked away, hidden. Disabled people were once perceived as bereft of hope, part of the walking dead. I now visit to make her visible and we talk, even though there is no response. I tell her of the family that grew after her separation, the wounds of internment and imprisonment, then the will to return and recover. I laugh at myself: Shizuko knows perhaps better than anyone about the will to sustain.

I then talk with some of the staff and gain more insights. I begin to learn some stories of how she survived and realize my mistake: she is far from expired. She lives to remind and to teach. I have to confront my prior beliefs and impressions of people with disabilities. I have to unlearn my assumptions and piece together the puzzle that easily cloaks this hidden world. We are all alive and full. Just listen.

I take a series of pictures of Shizuko as she rests, hoping to capture her in a peaceful pose. We have no portraits of her, a photo can make her real, evidence of her existence anytime during the past seven decades. Yet nothing can capture her narrative. A mere photograph will not dissolve the decades of invisibility. She shares an identity with those of the disability community, one of hundreds of thousands who remain in institutions and living in a world that doesn't see or seem to value them.

I reimagine my role as a writer and artist, someone who tries to reinterpret the biography of the frail old body before me, to see her world through the lens of the disconnected and yet distinct. A confrontation with an unseen world. A slightly out of focus depiction befits this character. Her pure white hair blends with the white pillowcases and sheets. She is shrouded in an old faded magenta blanket with a dingy color from countless washings and years of use. Her face is bony and skeletal, a slender arm peaks out from under the sheets. I hold a frail hand. Her knees are buckled and bent, a fragile body of history, a distinct angle of repose.

I've always imagined my family's history as a series of photographs. The image of my grandmothers as picture brides. The formal single portrait of my young grandparents dressed in their best Western clothes. A lone shot of an aunt in front of a garden and the wood carvings of my grandfather. Then nothing—I rely on governmental photos of random Japanese Americans during the World War II relocation—a child waiting for a train with a large paper ID tag hanging from her jacket button and a lost and scared look on her face. These photos tell a story my family was not alone. We have a few prints during my family's return to farming, including some blurry images of a farmer and his family in their fields. We have a sparse collection of us kids and cousins, Sansei playing in the dirt or working in family packing sheds during summer harvests. I keep one snapshot: in front of our old wooden farmhouse, my brother and I look like poor war orphans from Asia.

These black-and-white images provide a glimpse into an America and the contradictions we live with. They provide a simple history lesson of the everyday and ordinary life, not the grandiose and dramatic portraits of white America and stories of wealth and fame. The reality that we have so very few photographs speaks volumes. Few owned a camera and immigrants were typically not the subjects of photographers. We sought to maintain a low profile, isolated, alone in the countryside, out of camera range, the classic immigrant story of eking out a living and quietly planting roots.

Poverty and shame played a role: photos were for the rich and famous, for success and status. My family belonged to a class of the unseen and concealed, much like Shizuko before me. The body of an old woman. The smell of urine in an aging nursing home. The sounds of groans and agony fill the hallways. All natural and fitting. Just because I have no photo of Shizuko doesn't mean she has no history. This inconspicuous facility I had driven by for years—her room, her bed, her neighbors—all belong to an inaudible world she calls home, a place that quietly cares for her when no one else would.

Who captures the history and stories of the forgotten and invisible? The answer: those with the means to record the past and pass that down for others to accept as the truth. My calling is to bring light to this, not with a formal portrait but the reimagined snapshots of the everyday and commonplace.

I find an old photo, a bent black-and-white roll that could still be carefully unrolled and opened. Inscribed on this photo: "Camp Millwood August 18–25 1973." I had taken a week off from farm work to volunteer at a special camp for people with disabilities. We were between farm jobs; the stone fruit harvests were done, and we had yet to start raisins. I would be a counselor and share a cabin with a half dozen campers. It was my opportunity to explore.

The faces and voices returned as I studied the photo, but they were now somehow different fifty years later. I remember as I drove up to the site at Lake Sequoia in our nearby Sierra Nevada Mountains, I had no idea what I was getting into. During my years at our small, rural elementary school, I had witnessed little separation of other students with disabilities. We often shared the same classroom, ate together, played together, rode the bus together. I felt a limited sense of normalcy for that time in the 1960s, living in a world inhabited by tolerance and intolerance. We sat and laughed together in a fog of uneasy difference. Add a twist—the majority of us at my school were not white.

Scanning the photo, I recognized a few of the young men I had taken on a rowboat ride with on the lake. I recall listening to the campers talk about themselves and others. Fred talked to a cabinmate about watching out for Roger, another camper who needed a lot of help going to the bathroom and often had accidents. They seemed to ignore me as I was rowing and trying to keep the small boat stable. They talked and talked, nodded knowingly to each other. I was exhausted from rowing and asked if they wanted to try. We switched places and slowly rowed back to shore albeit without a smooth rhythm of arms pulling the oars in unison. We rocked and swayed in the water, sometimes going in circles but it didn't seem to matter, we eventually made it back to the dock.

The faces in the photo revealed a different understanding for me decades later. To be aware and yet oblivious to external definitions of what was normal. For a moment we all were fine. I shared this emotion as we struggled to farm organically and carve a niche for our small operation, spending decades trying to fit in, knowing well that our labors—like caring and nurturing a home for heirloom varieties of peaches and nectarines—would never belong in the large commercial marketplace. I thought of myself as guileless, but that trait should be applied to the campers: their character was filled with an innocence without deception. At this camp they could be themselves and momentarily ignore me and the outside world.

On the last night of the gathering, they held a dance with bodies swinging and bopping with a wild, whirling free spirit. One of the campers became hyperactive and slipped into a type of convulsion, like a seizure I had witnessed before at elementary school. I surprised myself by gently talking to Danny as he trembled and twitched on the ground, reassuring him everything was OK as others gathered around with concerned looks. Danny finally relaxed and the music started once again, and the dancing continued. Danny and I sat on a log bench to the side, then he nudged me to go dance again.

As I study that photo, I realize that all that week I was unable to flesh out the parallels of farming and caregiving. Both are testaments to time, resilience, interdependence, and community. But at that moment in my life and the lives of people with disabilities, we lived in a different reality. The quiet farmer in me sitting in the midst of a group photo of campers and counselors and surrounded by the smiling Freds, Rogers, and Dannys of our world. Soon after that group photo, we all divided and split into our separate worlds, invisible again.

We live with stories from the past that haunt us, a burden we endure often unconsciously. Many have lost the will to confront past injustices. My first step is to attempt to understand the strategy to endure. I'm guilty of living in a world of the comfortable, ignoring the context of history and how to cope with being American as a misfit. I search for images of my family's past to reframe our story and the integrity of our choices and actions. To imagine the unimaginable. To pause and wonder what has been hidden in the interiors of family cryptic messages that conceal the American betrayal against misfits—people with disabilities who did not look American.

To reconstruct imaginary memories and allow us to rehearse ways the world could be different. Reimagined memories not just to remember but to retrieve a new sense of the past and what may have been and what will be.

Gold Star Mothers. No one asks to be a Gold Star Family. You have a family member in the military service, they fight in a war and die, and only then do you receive the title.

I never thought about the meaning of being a Gold Star Family and never portrayed my Grandmother Masumoto as being a Gold Star Mother. Growing up, our family hid the photo of my Uncle George's memorial service. George Hiroshi Masumoto had joined the all-Japanese American 442nd Army Infantry Regiment and fought in Europe. He was killed on October 16, 1944, at Bruyères in northeastern France while fighting against fascism and for freedom. He was the eldest son in a family of six. The photo was taken in 1944 at Gila River Relocation.

I accidently stumbled on the photo one day when I was about ten. It was in my grandmother's dresser, stored in a drawer under clothes, tucked away with documents including her alien registration card and a handful of letters written in Japanese that she could not read, and some government documents. She had wrapped the photo with the letter from the army chaplain informing her of the death of her son and a small box that contained a Purple Heart. A yellowed white handkerchief protected the documents, bound together with a red ribbon and some fraying twine. When you farm and stay on your land, you rarely move, things are never purged, and instead are stored and hidden in a sacred spot for decades, undisturbed by choice.

I never met my Uncle George. He, along with thousands of others, had joined the 442nd regiment and battled Germans in Europe while their families were being incarcerated in America. I imagine his life was taken by honest German bullets that didn't discriminate between who looked like an American and who did not. My uncle, along with many, strove to prove their loyalty to the very country that had judged their parents and siblings as the enemy.

In the photo, two other Gold Star Families complete the portrait. One family has a son who's dressed in an active army uniform and holds upright the photo of his deceased brother. My family stands to the right side. My father, who had been drafted into the army earlier that year, also poses in uniform with his brother and sisters. My grandfather loosely holds the American flag as if he's unsure where to place his hands. My grandmother raises the photo of her dead son. She looks confused, sad, and crushed.

The situation confounds and astounds my soul. A Gold Star Family accepting the flag of a fallen son while held captive because of their faces. A Gold Star Mother loses her number one son and spends the rest of her life bewildered because America is where they take freedom away from you. Yet despite the racism, my family later returned to California, worked hard in the fields, and struggled to reestablish their identity as Americans.

An immigrant story defines our family. In the midst of the swirling turmoil of prejudice, they forged a life in this country they wanted to call home. As the politics of race continue to simmer in our nation, I pause as I study the photo of my family taken in the middle of the Arizona desert while locked up because they supposedly were not American enough.

I can now see a spirit of resilience in those faces: they sought a wholeness beyond simply happiness. They affirmed their place in this land and strove for acceptance. Despite all the attempts at exclusion, my family would not be marginalized: they fought for inclusion.

Shikata ga nai. It can't be helped.

This is the backstory behind a Gold Star Family. And my grandmother can now assume her place, recast with a sense of history that she is not alone and can join the ranks of Gold Star Mothers. She grieved for her son and a country she rightfully claimed as hers.

A single photo captures an unspoken history. Baachan Masumoto passed away in the 1990s. But I keep this photo that she once hid. When I go to the cemetery and visit her grave, I think of her face in the photo, alongside my grandfather. Perhaps only at a gravesite can I have the conversation that can lead to understanding and realize that the unexamined life is not worth living.

Shizuko belongs in our family photo album. I talk with her by her bedside. She lays quietly, shifting every once in a while. She understands and responds with an accepting silence.

Photos as a witness to history
even when there are none.

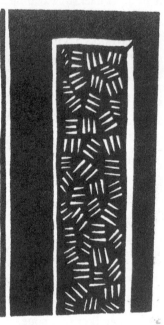

22

The Face of Anger

Spring adds an excitement of hope and potential on the farm. Our organic peaches and nectarines bloom boldly, heirloom varieties explode in complex blossoms with multiple petals appearing like miniature roses and layers upon layers of delicate pink tissue. Grapes push their leaves and reveal tiny bunches; we stop to count the miniature clusters to determine crop size and potential. We've opted to call most of our weeds with a softer term: "natural grasses." We have learned to live with most of these natural grasses, which create organic matter when ploughed into the earth and feed soil with life, instead of killing it with herbicides and poisons. These "natural grasses" belong on our farm. Life flourishes in the spring.

Shizuko bears the weight of how the disabled have been treated in the world. She has walked behind the walls of institutions and group homes, hidden from view, invisible to the public. Her life has been kept obscure; I'm reminded of the old phrase, "out of sight, out of mind." She now lays quiet and appears comfortable.

She lives. Not for a few days but rather weeks and months. I'm the one who is dense: it takes me a week or two to realize somehow, she must be fed and nourished. She could not survive without nourishment. She is not hooked to machines and IVs. Someone is caring for her.

Daily, the staff stimulates Shizuko to feed her. Their system is personal and intimate, devised by people who know her well and can engage with meticulous details. They rub the inner part of her chest by her arms, a mild irritation they know will stir her awake enough to consume nourishment. They do this daily "shaking" for weeks and weeks, starting with just fluids then progressing to a modified liquid diet. They call this "hand over hand"

feeding, and I wonder if, as time passes, Shizuko moves her own hands
responding to the comforting stimulation from familiar hands.

So she must "wake up" enough to be fed. She must respond to their touch.
The staff undertakes months of turning and rolling her body, rubbing her
joints and backside to prevent bedsores, shaking and stirring her awake to
drink nourishment in the hope she will return. They care and Shizuko is
learning to live again.

All the while, she is unresponsive to me. I am not present during her daily
feedings. I take comfort in the quiet, docile, still, and seemingly peaceful
Shizuko and do not see the active, anxious struggle to keep alive a ninety-
year-old woman. I am unable to provide reciprocity.

We are supposed to have that infamous family meeting. The conversation when
we challenge ourselves: how should we care for Shizuko? What are we supposed
to do about taking care of each other as we grow old?

I've been involved in a number of such meetings. One for Baachan Masumoto
when dementia overtook her life and she wandered away from home, escaping
back into a world partially here on our farm, then at my uncle's farm, my aunt's
home in town, and later to her childhood rice paddies in Japan. Another family
meeting involved my bachelor uncle when he had a stroke and alienated all his
siblings with mean-spirited behavior; I fell into the role of his caregiver by de-
fault. One more meeting took place with my parents who were planning their
wills, advance directives, and creating a family trust with the farm and their
small estate. But these family meetings were never easy. After my father suf-
fered a stroke and the questions you think you've covered were thrust into your
life, the family tried to collect their thoughts and plans while emotions ran wild.
Often, tensions arise and anger fills the gaps of the unknown.

But Shizuko is different. She carries the baggage of classified details we will
never know because we are not her guardians. Being family doesn't count in this
case; her caregivers do not need to consult with us, and they can and do proceed
to take care of her without our input. I'm not sure how we would have made decisions anyway. Who would have been granted authority? I review possibilities:
an uncle because of antiquated traditions of the lone male sibling automatical-

ly assuming decision-making; or the oldest surviving family member, my aunt, should assume responsibility; perhaps my mom since she lives the closest. Or me, from another generation and the one you could say "found" her—which is far, far from the truth.

The resulting family conversation would have been challenging. Emotions of blame, shame, and responsibility entangle with obligation and the years of separation. Different voices of love, guilt, and regret blend with the hope of reconciliation, forgiveness, and bonding. It's all intense because it's about family. We would all undergo a transformation, filling the gaps in our sense of history with what happened or didn't happen. It all expands and overwhelms us with life we can't see and yet, at the same time, we cannot unsee this body before us. The undefined dominates perspectives. We slip into nonaction, paralyzed by the circumstances, paradoxically comforted by the reality that someone else was caring for Shizuko. For years and decades. Without us.

The jolt is amplified due to the fact the family had worked hard to rebuild and overcome the racism of immigration and imprisonment, to rebuild lives. We all wore the appearance of success—educated, steady work, some wealth, and comfort. The ghosts of history linger like a shadow, even in the optimism of spring. We are reenacting the past, helpless, powerless. To make future plans assumes we have some level of control.

We are bonded by a shared baggage of history we cannot escape; many will press on and carry this burden. We have an attachment to the dreams of our immigrant parents and grandparents yet sense they are destined to be broken. A new precariousness slips into our lives. Our plans and hopes endure alongside the fantasy of what might have been. Emotions matter as feelings overwhelm and sometimes prevent us from doing good—we are trapped by what we are not. The painful optimism of an immigrant's tale awaits our fate—we will eventually fail and still survive. Yet Shizuko represents a communion with the forgotten, a reminder of the necessary contradictions in a family's history. We may stagnate and hunker down only to eventually forge forward, persist, and with luck, transform. So we beat on, pulled backwards into a sea of history, to reclaim childhood dreams, while at the same time, recapture the spirt of something that will never be.

While growing up, Baachan Masumoto, my father's mother, lived with us at different times. She was an Issei, and was also a woman farmworker who understood hard labor from working in the fields for decades. Her body hardened from the physical trials. Biceps bulged from her tiny four foot, six inch frame. She spoke little. Preferred the fields to friends. Quiet and reserved. She appeared pleasant and very serious about work. Growing up we never spoke the same language—hers Japanese and mine English—but we knew farm work, a shared stage for our family saga.

Yet once a year, she exploded. Her emotions shattered her quiet demeanor. I witnessed times when she snapped, her face tightened, and eyes grew narrowed and a scowl appeared. She began to wail; a low voice took over and she screamed in short bursts: "No . . . no . . . no." Then, in Japanese, she proclaimed things were wrong. Sometimes telling my father he was crazy to buy a farm. Other times she announced how they took everything from the family. They were wronged. They were wrong. They were bad. Her words didn't make sense yet rang with truth. She seemed ashamed of being Japanese yet knew all too well she was Japanese.

She would twist and turn her frame, stomping her feet, swinging her arms. A tantrum and seizure, an outburst and convulsion. We'd try to calm her, plead to decipher the problem, to be careful so she would not hurt herself. After a few long minutes, she often fell to the floor, beating the surface with her clenched fists, shaking her head back and forth. A spasm, a fit of anger, a hidden confrontation. She was condemned to her past.

Then she'd stop. We'd help her to her feet and sit with her. These were the only times I witnessed my father put his arm around her. They'd sit side by side, his arm embracing her body, a son cradling his mother, slowly rocking together as tears flowed down her face.

The war, the internment, the years behind barbed wire, a life of sacrifice, all exploded for a moment. We all knew little could be done other than to feel the silence and acknowledge the injustice. To bear witness and accept you are simply a kind of conduit—to make it real, to force the world to pay attention, tell the story of how we got here. Perhaps I would have to dispute all I had grown up to believe—that America was a just and safe world.

Shizuko lingers like a ghost shimmering as faint bands of light against a darkness. In the end, it's all about questions that haunt and provide comfort as we ponder. Gaman, or "to persevere." The security I've been granted in my lifetime hid the reality of our history. Shizuko becomes my teacher when I am ready.

Spring on the farm
and something is plowed into us.

23

Sunnyside

In the early 1970s, she comes home. Shizuko returns to the Fresno country-side during a dramatic shift in policy and attitudes about care. New federal and state legislation calls for decentralization and deinstitutionalization of large mental hospitals. Larger facilities witness a steady decline in popula-tion; DeWitt State Hospital is eventually closed in 1972. Shizuko's records show that she was then housed in numerous facilities in the Fresno area, one on Manning Avenue, about five to ten miles from our farm, and other places nearby, including the Sunnyside Convalescent Hospital, which also popped up on the list.

She discovers a rhythm of life. Everyday stories emerge about her per-sonality: she loves to tease and play tricks on staff. She likes to tickle them and gently pokes with her finger, then quickly runs away and snickers. She occasionally tries to trip those who care for her by suddenly sticking out one of her tiny legs when they walk by. She lets people believe she is a meek, innocent old lady but then pinches someone and quickly dashes back to her seat. She gets attention. And if she wanted someone's attention, she'd simply tug their hair. She was her own lady.

I hear stories about how if she is hot, she'd simply take her clothes off wherever she wanted. So the caregivers counter by giving her jump suits. She is a real character, her "own lady." She has a mind of her own, cap-tured in the comment: Shizuko does not dwell on the past and instead broadcasts an "I'm done with you" attitude. A happy, content character who openly displays her joy and energy.

She loves her morning coffee, gulping it down in a rush, like a kid who wants to quickly finish breakfast in order to go out and play. They try to slow her down because the coffee is very hot, but Shizuko doesn't know the meaning of being passive. Instead, the staff has to mix the coffee with cream or milk to cool the hot liquid—they adjust to Shizuko. After finishing her morning cup, she announces to the world that she is done by simply tossing the cup over her shoulder and behind her, often bouncing it off an unsuspecting diner. According to staff, they quickly learn to change her morning coffee ritual, serving the coffee in a paper or lightweight coffee cup and making sure there's a wall behind her. They ceased trying to change her. Shizuko chose to live in the moment and continued to toss her cup tomorrow and the next day and the next. She could dictate her future.

She loves music. Laughing and dancing, lifting her arms in the air and shuffling in a circle. She does not sing because she does not know the words, but instead giggles and grins, spins around and bumps into people. She seems to love gospel music, is entranced by a guitar accompaniment, claps out of rhythm, and taps her feet to her own beat.

She doesn't want to miss anything and is full of life. Occasionally, at her group homes, church programs are held. She attends, wanting to be part of the gathering. Often she falls asleep during the service but awakens to the music and springs up onto her feet.

If she wants something, she will sneak up and just take it, then promptly run away, laughing all the while. Later, if she realizes she did not want it, she will simply toss the object to the side and focus on her next caper. She is famous for tossing food that she doesn't want. While creating extra work for the staff, they claim her behavior is never with malice or anger. They seem to love her because she has life.

In a few, rare moments, she does speak. When touching someone, she might simply say, "Mama." The entire staff becomes her "Mama" as she scampers through the rooms, constantly in motion, cheerful. Her laugh is often like a whisper, "Ho, ho, ho . . ." She repeats, "Hai, hai, hai." (I believe the staff thought she is saying "hello" to everyone. Yet, perhaps, she is also speaking some Japanese—"hai" means "yes.")

They call her "Miss Sugi" or "Sugi." A character. Feisty. With a laugh. Even if she is tired, she naps for a minute but then returns by leaping up, *letting everyone know she is back. She becomes everyone's favorite, popping back to life all the time.*

Is she depressed? Seldom . . . if at all, I am told. If she doesn't feel good, such as when she catches a cold, she is simply less active. Most of the time, she is full of energy and scurries all over the place as if she's free to roam out in the open fields of nature, visible for all to see and feel. She makes life matter, contributing to the small world around her. Even when she breaks something—like an arm and she needs to wear a cast—it doesn't slow her down. She has mastered her own performance of pain, responding to frustration with her own intervention strategy.

Shizuko discovers a curiosity about life. She explores each new day, interested in every moment, snooping in all the rooms and hallways, searching contently. She initiates others into her world; they too learn to care for her. That's how she survives. She is the oldest patient with a disability on record in the Fresno region, surviving decades of life in institutions and group homes, shattering images of the erratic and inconsistent treatment of those who are disabled. She transforms. She turns inward to embrace intimacy over anger. Shizuko learns to love and be loved.

I've learned how to farm with failures. Organic farming required long learning curves, and I've discovered being Buddhist helps. I accepted a type of prolonged suffering but not in a Western and American sense of the word. I grew up not satisfied. Yet I did not long for something better, unlike the typical agribusiness mantra of a constant drive for efficiency, productivity, and expansion—crushing the little guy. Instead, we championed a quest for great flavor and taste, our definition of the perfect peach. That may have prevented me from becoming a great farmer with monetary success and political power. Instead, I have accepted what life threw at me. After farming for decades, I concluded that nature, like weather, will always win in the end—I could not control such forces. I accepted the power of nature. Later I realized nature included human nature. Inconsistency of behavior became part of our mantra on our farm. This sort of acceptance made our work fulfilling: to be part of a perfectly imperfect life.

Wabi-sabi. A Japanese concept that captured the beauty of things that were imperfect, impermanent, and incomplete. Our organic farm embodied this spirit. I later realized so does family. Shizuko seemed to live an imperfect life to the fullest. My family seemed to find comfort when they recognized our history was bound by wrongs. A mantra for both organic farming and people and their families thriving with a disability; the beauty of authentic life: imperfect, impermanent, and incomplete

Baachan Masumoto grew old with dementia. She was physically fit and still had muscle definition from farm work. She continued to perform well into her eighties. But as she aged, she often became disoriented. For years, she lived with us and occasionally packed her bags. She used an old black suitcase with the World War II family relocation number stenciled on the side: 40551. As she stepped out the back door, she would promptly announce that she was going home and began walking down the country road. We stopped and convinced her to return. "This is your home," I explained. The next day, she would attempt to leave again.

Our family was not unique. In this valley, the elderly remained and were often left behind in rural farm communities. Those of us who returned or stayed behind witnessed the aging of family members and their day-to-day descent. We are left to pick up the pieces and carry the burden of family as relationships are challenged and transformed, all the while wearing a "happy face" of what's supposed to be and ignoring what is.

After a series of family phone calls and meetings, my aunt in Fresno said Baachan Masumoto could live with her. This worked for a few weeks, until one day my grandmother walked to the bus stop, the same black suitcase in hand, and got on a city bus to "go home." A kind neighbor witnessed the escape and quickly followed the bus to the next stop, where my grandmother got off and was promptly returned to her residence. My aunt threw out the suitcase, hoping it would stop my grandmother. But it didn't.

Bewildered and overwhelmed with few other options, reluctantly the family decided to find a nursing home for her. They located one nearby where a handful of other older Japanese Americans were also housed. Of course, my grandmother then conspired with one of the other Issei women, and they both attempted to escape. They had to keep a strict eye on her. The name of the facility was Sunnyside.

I visited Baachan Masumoto often and noticed the other Japanese American residents. I vaguely recall a tiny white-haired woman with the name "Sugimoto." Marcy, my wife, was accompanying me once and pointed her out. I was informed that this Sugimoto was a wanderer, shuffling up and down the aisles, traversing past bed after bed like a zombie, always searching for something in the distance. But I was distracted and disconnected: I wasn't curious to find out who she was. I did not see this Sugimoto as family because I believed I knew all our family.

The stories of Shizuko swirl around me with each visit to her quiet room. Her history clashes with my sense of the past in ways I cannot comprehend. Contradictions. Discrepancies. Inconsistencies. Alienation. Shame. I live with them now, struggling to overcome my assumptions of what's supposed to be.

I think of our organic farm and the daily struggle to learn to work with nature and accept the uncontrolled and unanticipated—and the implicit bias I still carried: life was supposed to be logical, practical, and planned. Part of my brain wants to categorize Shizuko; the other is beginning to understand how unique she must be to have survived ninety years. With joy. Without us.

Complicated memories will blur with time,
mixing what I know with what I choose to remember.

24

Redress

Shizuko's language skills were altered at the age of five. From that point on, she could only say a few words such as "Mama" but never spoke a sentence or complete thought. It's easy to claim that she was robbed of a childhood— yet I wonder how she would have defined her life. Now, a silence lives in the room with the resting Shizuko. I wonder about the tales hidden in her mind, the conversations she never had, the fumbled opportunities to uncover how she truly feels and sees the world. The agony of untold stories churns within.

But her caregivers help to give her voice: some learn how Shizuko can still communicate in nonverbal ways by learning her rhythms and observing behavior. Shizuko finds champions to care for her. They share glimpses into her identity, who she became, how she engages in a performance over the decades they have witnessed. Their actions serve to partially rectify the misfortune heaped upon Shizuko. Perhaps their response to her condition helps to vindicate some of the abuses and circumstances of her past. They restore missing stories that can complete her. They define home.

Perhaps Shizuko doesn't just rest unconsciously. She may be dreaming, soaring and reimagining the consequences and impermanence of life. As she lays dying and living.

Shizuko disrupts the meaning of family obligations. Life has evolved since her departure in 1942. Her Issei parents struggled with challenges. Baachan Sugimoto raised her family as a single mother, witnessed her children depart, yet maintained a sense of family. The Nisei children bore the hardships of prison then returned to hostile homes in America. My parents, aunts, and uncles endured a plight that parallels Shizuko's journey: they cultivated a resilience my generation will never know. Survival demanded perseverance and acceptance. Like Shizuko, my parents' voices were often muted: they kept the unspoken hidden and protected within their souls.

Yet my family lives without regret. They carried a burden that protected my generation—I grew up in a muted and safe world. Only now do I begin to uncover stories that create twisted yet authentic ties that bind. Emotional mapping instills empathy alongside facts and details. Family histories are messy and complicated.

I remembered a book almost every Japanese American family seemed to own, even farmers like my father who rarely read a book or magazine. It was entitled *Nisei: The Quiet Americans* by Bill Hosokawa. It described the history of Issei immigration and Nisei experience including the relocation camps and World War II. The message in the book tended to be patriotic—how my family survived by being quiet and accepting their fate by demonstrating their loyalty. So my duty was to continue this legacy by being reticent. Leave it to others to tell our story.

Yet I often heard intimate stories not only from of my own family history but also the legacy of neighbors. Since I was one of the few Sansei to return to farming in our area, as the Japanese American farming community aged, I was given the task to write and deliver eulogies at dozens of funerals and memorial services. All my peers had left their family's farms. I witnessed their parents growing old, gradually weakening and then dying. Initially, husbands passed away and I would visit households to express condolences. Widows asked me to help with the Buddhist funeral arrangements. I often heard: "Could you say something about my husband? He was a farmer like you."

A eulogy gathers stories: remembrances and anecdotes, memories and reminders of a person's life. I was requested to add a voice to those who had passed. They were simple farmers, hardworking, reserved, often stoic. Yet as I listened, deeply personal stories poured out.

One farmer had an attachment to the land, to the orchards and vineyards. The surviving widow shared: "He was just an old farmer, handpicking grape bunches one by one, over and over. Grapes for the fresh market, grapes to dry into raisins. He shared life with others. The peaches and grapes carried his fingerprints, his story. He thought of the farm as his baby."

The ethic of work and partnership between a husband and wife. "Oh, how did we lift those sweatboxes full of raisins? They were over two hundred pounds, but we did it together."

A subtle message of inner strength and faith. "Somehow we managed after camps and relocation . . ." The widow looks down, unable to maintain eye contact. "It was hard . . ." Her voice trails off. Then a silence that captures the meaning of the moment.

Once I stopped and explained, "You should be telling your children and family these stories. They need to hear them and your silence, not just from me."

The widow paused, then with a slight grin she quipped, "Yes, but don't you want to be a writer? So you can tell them."

A classic moment of obligation, the gentle passing of a burden down to the next generation. She tricked me. I could only grin too.

But the silence motivates. Many Sansei did begin to search for answers, they challenged the forces of history and generational trauma and launched an investigation into the injustices of their family's and community's past. In the 1980s, a movement grew to confront the past in the present. To explore what we need to secure our freedom. To reclaim the denial previous generations carried and call it what it was: an American lie.

Redress was launched to help address the violation of rights perpetrated against the 120,000 Americans of Japanese descent who were forcibly imprisoned during World War II. A series of public congressional hearings were held, and dozens spoke of the pain and suffering. After a long political struggle and court cases, a congressional act was passed and signed by then-President Reagan.

I remember hearing about these hearings. Typically, soft-spoken Japanese Americans shared the emotions and trauma of being falsely imprisoned. They told tales of family challenges, self-doubt, and courage. Teams were formed to help the process, to assist in the quest to remember difficult and hard times. For decades, a people harbored secrets, carried a burden, and hid their faces. At the hearings, individuals shared the experience of the tens of thousands that brought their shame out of the shadows. To expose their fingerprints that tell a truth about America. The process validated deep emotions, allowing a people to begin the long trek to restoration and reconciliation. Only when these deeply personal stories were made public could the healing begin. It was a similar phenomenon that Jews experienced following the Holocaust: the need to tell stories publicly in order for a public healing to begin. Relocation and internment had branded a people with a public scar. It would then require a public sharing to mend the deep wounds. Trauma was not normal. To bear witness to the unspoken and bring light to the truth. To give voice to the silent. To demand others listen and to hear the roar from those who were muzzled and suppressed. Policy could be changed by fostering empathy when injustices were felt personally. A movement was generated: we no longer wanted to be quiet. We had voices. We were not America's problem; America was the problem. We were no longer your docile Japanese Americans. We now had a different story to tell.

My parents, aunts and uncles received a settlement check of $20,000. But what they cherished the most was the official presidential letter they received apologizing for the past. Their humiliation and shame was no longer private, our history no longer confidential. Their story was public and true healing could begin when others acknowledged the injustice. An atonement found in a simple piece of paper. My family were forgiven for being who they were.

A Letter from the President

My parents "knew" President Bush. It began with a letter of apology.

In 1988, President Reagan signed the legislation that granted reparations to Japanese Americans. Later, in 1990, President George H. W. Bush signed letters of apology, one sent to my folks.

I can remember opening the letter with my father. He silently read it and set it down. He said nothing. He closed his eyes for a moment, followed by a very subtle nodding of his head. He acknowledged the decades of pain and struggle; working silently in the fields; picking a peach or a grape bunch; invisible hands that fed a nation; luscious, sweet fruits that masked a lifetime of shame. With a nod, he felt a closure on a dark chapter in our family history: he accepted the apology from the president.

I thought about an honest relationship so rare in politics today. Of course, my parents had never met the president. They never talked with him nor even came close enough to shake his hand. But the letter carried the weight of something personal: it had meaning.

The current public discourse of politics has become polarized and divided. The idea of my mom forging a sincere exchange with a politician is foreign to her. Today, I can't imagine her receiving a letter of apology to right a wrong. Meaning seems absent in this political climate. Maneuvering and manipulation stands at the forefront, and a culture of fear and threats dictate who has the power. My family's quiet story of injustice would be overwhelmed in the sweeping noise of social media and the yelling and screaming.

Now perception rules. Messaging matters. Politics functions in the shadows. A simple letter that meant much to my father would never have happened in the present toxic world of political wars. He would have died with an open wound of shame.

The redress legislation from President Reagan and later the letter from President Bush was a public act of courage from both the Japanese American community and the politicians. My father then knew he had done no wrong. He had assumed the role of the head of household at a young age as his immigrant parents struggled to comprehend why they were branded as evil. He was later drafted and served in the US Army during World War II but rarely spoke of his service. He became a veteran of a private war against poverty and racism—a veteran of the invisible and forsaken. He worked hard to build a family farm in a country that had deserted him.

President Bush's letter began a public healing for him and a personal relationship with a president of the United States. The politics of that moment were sincere and honest and specifically directed to a quiet, reserved farmer, an American by birth, who simply wanted to know he was welcomed in this country he called home.

I think of Shizuko asleep and appearing peaceful. What redress does she have? She too should be eligible for the settlement and letter of apology. A court case should be filed, not only because of imprisonment of Japanese Americans and her internment in institutions but also the treatment of the people with disabilities. Their discrimination. Their injustice. Their pain and suffering. Their denial of rights. The revealing of her story, the voices of the disabled community matter. Shizuko's presence transforms into a chant: "Nothing about us without us."

Shizuko is not America's problem, America and attitudes and policies towards people with disabilities are the problem.

Exposure to acknowledge.
Unmasking empathy.

PART SEVEN

STRUGGLE
FOR ACCEPTANCE

25

Awakening

Shizuko wakes up. After months of inactivity, after weeks and weeks of sleep with her body stagnant in bed, after all she had been through her entire life, Shizuko awakens. She opens her eyes, sits up in bed, then gradually readjusts to life in her wheelchair. Slowly she returns to her typical, curious self, moving up and down the halls, never staying put. She grants herself an opportunity to be herself, an act of self-determination.

The staff is overjoyed to see her alive. She energizes them by never staying put. Sometimes when they feel tired with their routines, they assigned themselves to Shizuko and her spirit keeps them busy. They never get a rest break but time with Shizuko flies by. She fills their days.

One staffer tells me: "When I get a little down, I think of Sugi. I think that if Sugi can get through life, what do I have to complain about?"

They quietly have coined a motto: "Be a Sugi."

After her awakening, she continues being present at the assisted care facility.

"She loves to be tickled; her tummy is the most sensitive."

"We're not surprised, she was too full of life to leave us."

"She came back home."

She roams the facility, pulling her frail seventy-pound body down a corridor, grabbing the handrail and pushing with her feet.

One staff person tells a story: "When I first met this tiny old woman, I said, 'What a sweet lady.' She then promptly entered my office and messed up everything on my desk, then escaped while giggling. Such a character and only seventy pounds."

Her silver and white hair flows. Occasionally they tried to pull her hair up and out of her face, but Shizuko doesn't like it. She promptly pulls out the rubber bands along with some strands of hair and tosses them to the floor. She insists her hair be loose and free.

And now she somehow recovers from her stroke after being bedridden for months, her life restored by caregivers. The family can reunite with a lost sister and aunt. Sort of.

The family found Shizuko because of death. When she had her stroke, most everyone assumed this tiny, ninety-two-year-old woman would pass quickly. She had been assigned to hospice care. Due to some remaining funds annually allotted to her while a ward of the state, a basic life insurance policy had been purchased to cover her funeral expenses. That's how Ranee from Wild Rose Funeral Home became involved, which led us to Shizuko, after seventy years of separation.

Viewing Shizuko in what we thought was her final phase of life felt as a fitting end to her life story. As she lay in bed, her body gently curled and seemingly unaware of us, the silence felt proper, the stillness right and moral. We felt a closure. Her case closed. But she then awakens and we ask: "Now what?"

When we had gathered around her earlier, could she hear the hum of human voices, the voices of family? Did she awaken one last time to be with family? But it's unclear if she could hear us. Now, after she had risen, would she recognize us?

I walk in and see an empty bed. A phone call from the staff had informed me that Shizuko is conscious and alert, now in her wheelchair. I find her shuffling down the hallway, wandering and exploring. As I approach, she turns and looks up at me. Then, as I get closer, she gently kicks me in the leg.

She holds up her foot. Her shoe needs adjusting; the strap has come loose, and one lace is twisted and tangled. She seeks help, something our family had resisted—part of a Japanese ethic of not seeking assistance and thus not creating a situation of obligation and the need to repay someone for their help. I stop to adjust Shizuko's shoe. She then drops her leg and continues her journey down the hall as if beckoning me to follow. I stand and watch then shake my head. She had just kicked me!

We had prepared for her funeral, not for her living. The meaning of family has been challenged. Shizuko scours the facility corridors. These hallways carry no meaning for me; I have no history here where she has lived for decades. Yet she seems to be foraging for something, revisiting places, rummaging her memories, searching.

I think of my Baachan Masumoto in her final years out in the country. I once wrote about her in one of my stories.

As if walking against the wind, she would slouch forward and plod along the earthen trails. Her frail, eighty-year-old legs shuffled through the soft dirt, creating puffs of dust that marked her path. She'd clasp her hands behind her, shoulders round, her tiny frame silhouetted against a brilliant orange setting sun. I can picture her trudging through fields she worked but never owned. I believe that despite a life of poverty and the crushing upheaval of the World War II relocation, in her old age she found peace during those farm walks, covering familiar territory and finding a place where she finally belonged.

Shizuko too scouts her pathways, investigating the corridors, probing the terrain. I imagine her on a farm walk from her childhood, freely wandering through the orchards and vineyards, combing through her memories. I follow in her footsteps, confounded and bewildered while reflecting and meditating.

I continue to visit with the staff. They are open to sharing stories, filling in the blanks of her life. I interview some of her case workers. One knew Shizuko since she first came home to the Fresno area in the 1970s. Another has cared for Shizuko with a truly giving heart, accompanying her on outings. Many of the staff adopted her as their own: they are the outstretched arms that keep her from falling. Because of them, Shizuko has outlived all the other patients.

They call her "Miss Sugi" and not by her first name or last name. "Sugi" was her nickname but not a name she used as a child nor a familiar moniker any of her family had coined. Most Nisei understood the act of acquiring names; they had Japanese names at home but once they began school as children, they were randomly assigned an American name by a teacher who blatantly believed they knew better. My father went to school as a "Takashi" and came home as "Joe." It was now part of the name he had to accept along with the face he wore.

I listen and take notes about Shizuko's life. The tales are stunning. Unrecorded moments, often about the so-called "misfits" of history, these tales bring shame out of darkness and deliver light upon the dynamics of race and poverty and disability. The voices build empathy about Shizuko's life and the challenges of class discrimination. Her facility is filled with them, hidden out of sight. Within these walls their stories lie dormant, waiting to be exposed should someone inquire. Race matters: the majority of her caregivers are people of color. They sense a deep culture of compassion; their actions epitomize an authentic exchange and not sympathy for those in need. To love and be loved, Shizuko finds an identity.

These are recuperative memories that history can't tell. Typically, we bury a brutal past, try to forget and move on; accept being the victim and not a survivor. This is how traumatic memory works: to be caught in the pitched battle between remembering and forgetting. Instead, I want to remember. I have no direct memory of relocation, of internment, of departure and dislocation. The repressed memories mask my own separation of history, the fear of my generation to pose disruptive questions of the past. Instead, we allow the extra space for ghosts to wander, displaced and homeless. They challenge us to forget. Forgetting is the other invisible half of history. Sometimes to accept the past is to forget.

I am transformed but not in the manner I expected. A few of the staff eye me as the stranger I am. These caregivers are often underpaid, overworked, tasked with caring for the old and forgotten as the rest of the world drives by refusing to see them. I too have been guilty and blind to such an indiscretion. I must learn to respect the distances that I can never overcome and still accept being part of family. Maybe. One worker is brutally honest and when I announce I am Shizuko's nephew, he casually yet bluntly says, "Where have you been for all these years?"

Shizuko is mostly surrounded by caring people and a culture that create a

home. They love in a manner I do not fully comprehend. A love that fright-
ens; something we need the most and dread the most because it exposes
contradictions.

I follow Shizuko down the hallways and corridors. A cruel revelation: to accept
fate, to affirm destiny, to respect distance, to recognize resilience. We did not
discover Shizuko: she found us. And we are not her only family.

The family is shaken again. One by one they come to visit with Shizuko, to see
her alive and awake, in constant motion, moving away from us as she scoots and
scurries down the passageways. This transition will take time, to learn more of
her stories and an incremental grasping of the past.

We try speaking to her in Japanese, wondering if she will respond, perhaps
something from her past could be stirred. It is a language she had not heard
in seventy years. Some family members claim Shizuko responds, turning her
head to a familiar language, a voice from the past. Yet, I am not sure. She
certainly senses our presence but without recognition. She does seem to thrive
with the attention.

Throughout her life, Shizuko discovered a way to inhabit a future. She awakens and we're forced to confront a living testament. She represents forces in the
past that are alive and impactful now. She survived in her own world, yet her
story is now part of our world. History becomes part of who we are and what
we can become. We cannot forget the faces we wear and the color of our skin.
Perception and reception.

Is Shizuko well? Was her life wasted with regrets and the would haves, should
haves, could haves? Her awakening brings shock but also joy and a treasure. We
can see her alive in the context of her own world.

Shizuko lives as a subject of history and not an object. We are compelled to
speak of her in the present not past tense. She is visible. She empowers us to reclaim our family's place in the history of immigration, wars, discrimination, and
prejudices. She awakens and we wake up to the past in the present; we are active
participants in recasting a family epic we can no longer deny. I've taught myself
to forget. I now force myself not to look away. Others too must witness and not
turn their attention away in order to redefine the world in convenient ways.

Much of the past has been buried and I am beginning to understand the forces that contributed to silence. I cannot change our faces, but I can claim ownership and the challenges as my family tried to carve a future in a foreign land. We are American and Japanese. Shizuko is a survivor and a person with a disability. Her actions demand we accept her for what she is and not what she isn't. We are part of an active participant as we forge our own histories. We can demand agency. We plan for the future because we can imagine life in the future. America needs to accept and change, not us.

Shizuko has returned to complete a cycle of reunion and redemption by being herself. She helps us to both remember and move on, to forget and return, to return to the real world where it's OK to be ourselves. Her voice remains subdued, restrained, perhaps, by my own limitations. Yet her presence enlightens us, and we are forced to ask and ponder. To bear witness and consent, then acknowledge.

You can't choose your family.
But you can choose to remember.

26

Tōrō Nagashi—Floating Lanterns

The Tōrō Nagashi *ceremony marks the end of the* Obon *season, a Japanese tradition celebrating the belief that our ancestors can return to this world once a year to visit family and their home villages.* Obon *begins with an annual summer dance festival when bright lights and lanterns are hung and rhythmic music and dancers in bold colors entice the ghosts of family members to reappear and reunite family. A few weeks later,* Tōrō Nagashi *marks the end of this commemoration—small lanterns and candles are mounted on miniature boats or rafts and set into a stream during the late evening to take the spirits back to their otherworldly homes.*

As if she too is an ancestor returning at Obon, *Shizuko recovers to roam the halls of our lives. It's summer harvest time on the farm, so I squeeze in visits with her between workdays. I learn more of her story from staff and by simply observing. She now rolls in her wheelchair for hours and hours. She has discovered a routine to immerse herself, a daily crusade to move forward and explore, to comb the corridors and propel herself. She has learned how to let go of her disabilities and doesn't seem to worry about others nor even herself.*

I don't feel ignored. We acknowledge each other, not like aunt and nephew, but rather as people. Occasionally, she looks up to me and signals she needs help to nudge her chair along, turn a corner, maneuver around another wheelchair or past an open door. She grips the handrails as she rests, then resumes paddling her tennis shoe-bound feet, tiny step after step, down another trail and trial. She has returned and rejoins us in this world.

Every summer we harvest our organic peaches, nectarines, apricots, and then grapes for raisins. Heat dominates, rain is rare; the fruits thrive in this environment. They grow sweet with each passing day. We monitor daily, even hourly, to capture their peak of maturity in order to pick and pack the fruit precisely at the right moment. Emotions run high with expectations and anticipation. We have learned that nature dictates timing. High maintenance is demanded with amazing rewards waiting for those who invest time, energy, and effort. We are renewed with each harvest.

In the middle of our fruit season, *Obon* begins, and I welcome our ancestors back to our farm. In Japan, *Obon* is only a three- or four-day event, but here in the San Joaquin Valley of California, it has morphed into a three- to four-week celebration. Each small town with a Buddhist temple hosts their *Obon* dance on consecutive weekends. I grew up looking forward to visiting the neighboring temples of Fresno, Fowler, Reedley, Visalia, and Parlier. I dance in the streets and temple grounds as Japanese songs echo throughout the neighborhood and hundreds gather displaying community spirit. It was a welcomed break from the grueling farm work. I imagined ancestors extending their stay on the Japanese American family farms scattered throughout the valley.

Recently in Fresno, we have added *Tōrō Nagashi* to demark the ancestors' return to their homelands, a relaxing moment at dusk to wish them bon voyage and a safe journey. Typically, in early August, as our tree fruit picking slows, we enjoy a natural break before the raisins begin in September. For my family, *Tōrō Nagashi* coincides perfectly as if it was planned according to our organic harvests. *Tōrō* in Japanese means "lantern," and *nagashi* translates into "cruise;" my interpretation: "beacons sailing into the night."

We reserve a lantern for my father who passed away in 2010. His name is written on the miniature paper shrine with a candle inside. It's mounted on a small raft, and we gently launch the craft into the water, allowing him to return to the afterlife. I am also thinking of Shizuko—who had not yet passed but she too seems to be looking for a path home, a misfit seeking the fields where she is accepted. In the future, we will dedicate a lantern to her.

My late father left his mark on our family farm. He and I worked side by side for forty years before his stroke. His spirit lives in the grapevines he planted with my uncle in the early 1950s. They were establishing a new vineyard. Their father was helping in the barnyard, cleaning and trimming the cuttings that had been carefully growing from the prior year when new roots were established. Now they were hand planting them in the fields.

My older brother was helping our grandfather; my sister had just been born and I was to come two years later. My grandmother was inside the farmhouse with my infant sister while my mom was out in the fields tying vine canes to wires. They tell me that my brother was fluent in Japanese, the three-year-old chatting with his grandparents who also lived with us. Suddenly my grandfather stopped, gasped for air, and slumped over, suffering a heart attack. My brother desperately tried to awaken his grandfather then dashed into the house to alert his grandmother. She ran out into the fields to call her sons and my mom.

Alone, my brother tried to help. He pushed a chair up to the kitchen sink, grabbed and filled a glass with water, then carefully carried it out to his dying grandfather. He tried his best by sharing water, hoping it could help bring back life. The others sprinted home, but it was too late; my grandfather had died. After the funeral, my brother stopped speaking in Japanese. He ceased to convey messages from one generation to another. He does not recall ever knowing the foreign language.

As I work that vineyard, I contemplate this origin story and the spirits that join me with each time I pass down a row and each grape I pick. That's why *Obon* comes so naturally to our farm. During each summer harvest, I can stand on the shoulders of those who came before me.

We also farm a block of fifty-year-old, fully producing Sun Crest peach trees, an "old growth forest" by modern standards of commercially grown fruit. I helped plant that orchard with my father. I was an anxious teenager helping the old farmer. My father's rows are straight; my rows are slightly crooked, and I'm reminded of that with every tractor pass down the row when I have to swerve around crooked trees and make an adjustment.

I have kept this old, heirloom variety even though it sometimes struggles in the current marketplace due to its golden color when ripe instead of the antic- ipated bright red of modern peaches I'm told that consumers are demanding. Also add an assumption about short shelf life and occasional odd shape which create a twisted perception of "what is a defect?" These implicit biases in life challenge us all. Each harvest, echoes of my family's ghosts compel us to find a home for these homeless fruits.

With each *Obon* season, I think of the countless contributions of farmwork- ers who have also labored on our farm, including those who have pruned the one-hundred-year-old grapevines in front of our farmhouse. Their hands too shaped these vines. I can feel the pruning scars from generations before me. I can map the separate blocks of trees and vines, each with a story of their found- ing—grapes on higher ground since they demand less irrigation water, early season nectarines on sandy soil because we will not hang a heavy crop, and an heirloom peach on our best soils to enhance the depth of their flavors. Genera- tions of hands continued to shape and structure each vine and tree like a sculp- ture, a friendly reminder of the ghosts that haunt our fields.

Many of these hands belong to the forgotten and invisible. Every summer in the 1960s, migrant workers came for a summer harvest, then left for apples in Washington in the early autumn. Often these workers spent winters in Texas. I can recall old cars with Texas license plates driving into our backyard in spring. Families were seeking work and for months they joined our operation.

They brought more than their labor. As a kid I remember the young men and women, perhaps only teenagers, singing a new cool sound of Tex-Mex music from the Sir Douglas Quintet, Little Joe, or Sam the Sham and the Pharaohs. These sounds crossed borders and connected our little town of Del Rey with the South Texas towns of San Antonio and El Paso. This music visited our small farm summer after summer. At the end of harvest, they'd load up their cars, drop by the house for their final checks and we'd wave goodbye. Their songs then joined my rock and roll *Obon* repertoire as I imagined dancing to a different beat.

I farm with these spirits eternally. Each left behind something more than success: they bestowed us with significance. As I conclude another season, I begin to understand the sense of accomplishment of my grandparents, parents, aunts, and uncles. Each harvest proved they were accepted here in America. They labored an entire year, trusting that the fruits they grew could find homes, would bring them a livelihood, and help them plant roots in this new land. With the presence of the ghosts of misfits and those marginalized, I can foster an integrity, creating a world I want to be part of, feeling the past in the present. I do not farm alone. I participate on a mental time travel journey, re-envisioning tradition as something real and visceral, granting me the agency to plan for the future, part of an examined life worth living.

Each family carries their memorial raft to the waterside and gently launches it. In Japan, these crafts are often placed in a small stream or brook, and they smoothly sail away downstream and eventually out to sea. In Fresno, we utilize a small lake and on a typical late summer evening, a gentle breeze shimmers over the surface, guiding the lanterns gently out onto the water, drifting in the wind away from the shore.

I watch them flow out away from the banks. Most gather in a line, floating along a track in the blue waters. A few though strike out on their own, lingering, as if not wanting to depart, tempted to remain with the other before meandering away on a different path. One of those lone lanterns

symbolizes Shizuko and the unknown forces pushing her raft astray, jour-
neying on a different route unique to her.

Shizuko came to life and visits us. She brings her motion and energy.
She is a living ancestor, awakened to illuminate. She no longer lives in the
shadows and now steps into the light of family and our history. I am slowly
grasping her sense of a future defined by the past.

Japanese have searched for acceptance in America. The pace of this journey remains slow. Now the next generation witnesses the lanterns drifting into the
darkness.

My two children grew up on our family farm and now, as adults, they are partners in our farm operation. They experienced a unique and wholesome childhood—filled with playing in dirt, living with nature around them, knowing the
forces that generated extremes in weather and markets. These all contributed
to memories and a resolve that will continue later in life, a spiritual engagement
to the natural world around us all. I did not leave in the morning for a distant
office for my daily work. My family was never far from old-growth vineyards
and orchards established many decades before their arrival. They shared in a
history of place that anchored their sense of place. Our hope is moored in an
experience that remains alive, much like the ghosts of ancestors who have left
their mark on this place we call home.

My family had to remake themselves and accept destiny, to know who they
were and were not. Others had a power to determine what we remembered. All
I can do is to corroborate with story, clinging to a belief: you can't change the
past, but it's noble to try. How can you break the ties that bind us yet acknowledge and accept the baggage of the ancestors? At times we run faster to escape
the past so that love can remain pure and simple. Driven by emotions, we ignore
the realities of the world, stretch out our arms further and find joy. Close my
eyes, I make a wish to see the world differently.

The whole family participates in the Tōrō Nagashi festival. Our children,
now adults in their twenties, help launch the lantern bearing their grand-

father's name. As we look out at the hundred floating candles, we can hear the voices of many drifting away until next year. Each carries their own story of what might have been and what path was taken. Marking the event with generations expands our sense of time: spirits soar with the presence of the next wave, a harvest of new dreams that will be realized as new stories are written. The arc of Obon connects with a near and distant future. Small waves churn on the shoreline in a seemingly endless repetition as the lanterns drift away from us.

One day, Shizuko's small raft will wander from the flotilla, and I will smile at the significance. My imagination runs wild with the image of spirits guiding and nudging, manifesting the forces of history in her life and now our life. We are all still seeking a home where we are accepted as who we are.

The present-day rhythms of life move at a frantic pace. We live in a constant blur. It's easy to forget the past and instead only strive to move forward. Clinging to yesterday is perceived as a disability. Innovation and change rule. Historical amnesia is rewarded. Commerce and business drive life. To be successful, farms must become factories. Discard the shovel for chemicals. Replace human hands with machines. Supplant memory and experience with data and technology. The farmers' annual dance with nature is replaced by an algorithm and spreadsheets driving profitability. Returns on investment are based on economic value and ignore human capital. The ghosts have no place in this brave new world.

Our countryside is emptying of most Japanese Americans. The family farm legacy is disappearing like a sunset on the horizon. Many look to the east and a new sunrise. My life as a Sansei was built on being safe. Assimilation provided the path for success for children of immigrants. I joined a new arena of opportunity and pursued the perceived signs of success.

The cycle was complete when my children, the fourth-generation Japanese in Ameria, the Yonsei, were born. Their world exploded with new energies and the new harvests that rewarded those who dared to venture. The optimism of another harvest season has arisen.

The first generation Issei, have passed away. The Nisei aged and are transformed into silent witnesses. They wore masks in order to accommodate and adjust. Some carried the guilt of the survivor but rarely passed it on to the next generation. We Sansei retreat into a safe and protected world based on security. We will never taste hunger. We complete the arc and are now American.

Or not. We should tell the truth about ourselves that will release us into a new possibility. How quickly we became white, and I don't want to be white. The realization that suffering of the past feels distant while the future remains elusive, still out of our control. Yet we cannot escape our beginnings.

For my children, maturing in a rapidly changing world, innovation forces new thinking and a vision to see what's really there. The face of America has expanded. Inclusion becomes possible. Many of this generation are born with a freedom to dream and leave. They have agency despite living in a country that minimizes trauma.

Yet we recognize pockets of the past remain entrenched. Progressive ideas have abandoned rural America and our communities too often slip into nostalgia and reactionary thought—a longing "for the good old days," which ignores the fact that the "good old days" were not that good for many, especially Japanese Americans, people of color, women, people with disabilities, and other wrongly named "misfits" who were not accepted and did not belong, like weeds. The ancestors of some did not welcome strangers from a distant shore.

> *The lanterns illuminate the evening sky. Together they cast light contrasting the growing darkness. We watch as the candles begin to flicker, the wicks gradually reaching their ends. One by one they go dark, the light vanishes, and all is forgotten. Yet we know the light will continue to travel, disperse outwards, expand to the heavens. Only by letting go can I see the invisible waves soar.*

Ancestors return.
They have found home.
Will I?
Work to be a good ancestor.

27

The Great Fair

Shizuko loves going to the fair. She had full use of her legs and scurried around, a churning ball of grit and energy.

Every October, the Fresno District Fair is held at the fairgrounds on the edge of the city limits. Like most county fairs, it originated as a post-summer harvest celebration of agriculture, a moment of fun and amusement. Gradually a carnival and exhibition section were added with the promise of adventure and thrills along with the opportunity to renew old friendships and be exposed to new experiences.

Shizuko and a small group from her assisted care facility annually visit the fair with their chaperones. Because she is so active, Shizuko requires her own attendant. She enjoys the cows and goats and wants to reach out and pet them all. She likes their aroma, the feel of nature, the sense of being outdoors and free. The animals also seek attention, and she touches as many as she can. Perhaps she journeyed back to the farm with each fair visit.

She is very curious about the "freaks of nature" on display in the carnival section, especially the odd creatures like the six-legged sheep or the two-headed turtles. Shizuko's escorts have to be careful and nudge her to move on, otherwise she will linger for a long time, staring at and scrutinizing the oddities. She doesn't like to be interrupted while studying the "misfits" of nature, enthralled by their imperfection, enchanted with their incomplete souls, seeing something most others are blind to. She embodies a courage of acceptance.

At other times she is a "terror," I am told, exploring the new sights and sounds—"curious and a handful" is how she was described. She tries to bolt from exhibit to exhibit, pavilion to pavilion, speeding down the walkways and squeezing through the crowds, her helpers always monitoring so she doesn't get away. She requires her own posse to keep up. She knows what she wants to see.

Throughout my life, especially when I was younger, our family always went to the fair. It was the blend of "country traditions" with the ag pavilion showcasing our valley's produce bounty; the cow barn and small animal exhibition of rabbits and birds; the home arts building that housed the baked goods and preserves along with the quilts and table-setting displays; and of course, the carnival rides and fair food we had to eat once a year.

I can recall watching other people—a band of seniors from a nursing home, some with canes and some in wheelchairs, and the large family with parents attempting to herd children together. Occasionally a group of people with disabilities stand out. They'd be clustered as a clan, shuffling slowly, maneuvering with uneven gaits, often holding hands under attendants' watchful eyes.

They seemed to wind through the grounds, carving out their own invisible path. Actually, when others noticed, the crowds stepped to the side, got out of the way and allowed the crew to pass by, both acknowledging them with a goodwill gesture yet avoiding them. As soon as the band passed, the crowds merged back together and mingled again. They recognized the group of people with disabilities only to ignore them once they passed by.

At the Fresno Fair, I sometimes followed groups of kids and adults with disabilities as they trekked through the grounds. The group explored all the sights with their eyes and senses, at times staring wildly at all the attractions, other moments they seemed almost overwhelmed with the crush of people and sounds. Some wanted to reach out and touch it all while others stayed close to the chaperones, clinging to each other, holding hands, and clutching arms. Yet they all looked happy. Empathy, not sympathy was what they sought. They hoped for connection, not separation.

Once, I watched a group consume some cotton candy. They hesitated at first, not sure how to eat the puffy treat, but they quickly started grabbing and devouring the pink cloud, laughing and giggling with a sugar high. I remember their faces and bodies: they embraced a joy, a moment of pure pleasure.

As I grow older, I think about that moment, finding it harder and harder to mimic such an act in my own life. Of course, I overthink, wondering if it is joy or a type of simple acceptance I had observed.

Stories of the fair makes me think about the hidden history: these grounds served as an "Assembly Center" in the first half of 1942 for thousands of Japanese Americans who lived west of Highway 99. Those who were living in this "restricted zone" were deemed dangerous and were forced to move to the horse stables and temporary barracks set up at the fairgrounds racetrack from May to August. My mom tells the story that since our family lived east of Highway 99, we were in the "free zone" and not incarcerated at that time. (But by August 1942, all Japanese Americans were evacuated and imprisoned). So during that summer of '42, she'd go to the fairgrounds and visit a friend. My mom was free to enter and leave while her grammar school friend remained a prisoner.

Hearing the stories of Shizuko at the fair prompts a conclusion: many of us were "misfits"—we were poor, not white, not Christian, and different. To belong, we accepted our place and became second class and invisible. The American Dream as a land of opportunity is not equally dispersed; it is out of reach for most. The pit of inequality is always there. Yet the next generation will step into a world with a different confidence; the potential of a free and open world seems to beckon. Finding space at the margins will provide us a place to see America clearly.

Money could have changed history. When Shizuko contracted meningitis, antibiotics were first introduced on an experimental basis and available for a select few. But the poor had no access to such advancements and the medical world was segregated, often by race. So we accepted who we were.

If our family were wealthy, they could have escaped internment by traveling east of the Mississippi. Or to an island in the Caribbean. Imagine if I was raised on a tropical island: we could have farmed different crops, hidden in paradise.

Or with money, our family could have been rescued by travelling, ironically, to America's paradise: Hawaii, where most of the Japanese American population was not interned. I heard stories that during World War II, when Japanese Americans from Hawaii joined the 442nd, the all-Japanese American infantry battalion of the US Army, they were shocked to hear about the relocation camps. They could not believe families of fellow soldiers were locked up while their sons fought for freedom.

Money can buy love. Or it could help us at least escape so love could remain pure and simple, driven by emotions, as we ignore the realities of the world. Then we can run faster and stretch our arms further and find joy.

But the headwinds and tailwinds of history push and pull us in different ways and along different paths. My calling is to challenge the lies of the past: to act while dreaming and attempt to connect, like the child of immigrants who long to return to the homeland only to discover home was always here in America. My family became farmers and planted roots in the land that called them the enemy. Shizuko journeyed along a different trail and survived to share a wisdom no one would have expected: it's OK to be herself. When our paths aligned, I discovered that she was still alive at ninety-four and had survived decades of institutionalized care.

We all worked to escape the past and yet, somehow, accept it: to run from the ghosts and simultaneously reach out to embrace them with gratitude. To journey, to reclaim our stories, boats against the current, though failure and death await you; a new vision of nostalgia blended with meaning, pulling the past forward so we can take on new opportunities as we try to connect the dots of our past and make sense of the future in the present. Not to judge but to understand.

The walls of prisons surround, no escaping the memories.
But a will to ask questions to hear stories that can free us.

28

Caregivers

Shizuko knows them well. They take care of her. They respond to her daily pinching antics and tripping pranks. They do not prevent her from wandering down the hallways nor stop her walking routines. They love her and she accepts their love.

They work behind the scenes. They are underpaid and undervalued for the care they give. They receive little respect. They are often like Shizuko, children of immigrants, people of color from low-income households.

Acts of kindness. Pay it forward. Compassion in daily life. With caring comes courage. The Buddha: "After enlightenment, the laundry."

I share some of our organic peaches to thank the staff who take care of Shizuko. I set twenty boxes of peaches on a counter, a couple hundred pounds of our best fruit, hoping they'd accept a small act of gratitude for their years of service.

The staff doesn't know what do to with the gift. Some stop and inquire why the crates are sitting at their workstation, as if it were a mistake. I try to explain. They do not understand that they were gifts. Few thank me. I am disappointed. One then explains: they rarely get gifts for caring.

I stumbled on a new term called "job crafting" to describe the ways workers utilize opportunities to redefine their jobs and change their tasks and interactions with others. One report examined hospital cleaning staff who often went beyond their job description of mopping floors and cleaning rooms of patients. Many crafted new boundaries and definitions of their tasks into something much more meaningful for themselves and others. For example, one worker rearranged wall prints weekly, hoping the change of scenery would help the long-term recuperating patient to be stimulated, perhaps sparking something to speed healing. Another worker diligently mopped the floors of a patient's room. When the family returned to visit and was told bad news, they took out their anger and yelled at the custodian to come back and clean up the floors. He quietly returned, knowing his actions could help the family cope and accept a negative turn of events. These workers went beyond following orders, they understood the power of informal acts and redefined their duties. Some renamed their titles: "I'm an ambassador of the hospital," or "I'm a healer with a mop." They did what was right, not what was expected.

These were the caregivers that surrounded Shizuko—restoring her life, granting her a freedom to live, insuring she did not struggle alone. They were often invisible, unsung, and hidden. There were no group photos of this stand-in family posted on a wall above Shizuko's bed. I did not learn of their history unfolding a few miles from our family farm. I missed their guiding power that now seemed magical.

Our daughter, Nikiko, is partnering with me on the family farm. She is assuming responsibilities, carrying out daily chores and work duties of pruning, thinning, and harvesting fruits. She is adding a new relationship to the farming culture we have tried to create: a culture of caring, farmers as caregivers to the trees and vines and to nature. That's how we try to farm organically: to take care of the earth, the soil, the environment. But also to take care of the workers and the systems surrounding the foods we eat, to nourish not only our bodies but our souls, to take care of the family on the farm.

The caregivers surrounding Shizuko would have worked well partnering on our organic farm. We both build worlds out of small ambitions. We refuse to be worn out. We accept life does not always go the way we wish yet we beat on with fragile optimism. We can imagine a land anew.

I discover a credo the best caregivers emulate: focus on the immediate. They are not worried about how Shizuko got there. They do not worry about the conundrums that hide in each person and families that may never appear. They attend to her day-to-day care. They do not passively tolerate her antics; they recognize her as a person and engage with her. They see a future no matter how limited or confined the present feels. They labor on to advance Shizuko's memory.

I struggle to identify the real Shizuko. She has been awake for months. I learned of her presence for almost a year, yet I still see her disabilities and carry a burden of what could have been and should have been. I am slow to learn from the caregivers who treat the human and not the disease. Yet I know not everyone in Shizuko's circle of care from her past has been understanding and worthy of praise. The system has many flaws, vastly under resourced and over-stretched. Many tried to do their best within a structure that lacks sufficient support—these workers are disgracefully forgotten and sadly cast away, much like the patients they are assigned to care for.

I bear a shame entangled with denial. I am intertwined with my family's silence that has bound us in ways I am only uncovering as I grapple with generational trauma. Like Shizuko, I am finding my way and living in an imperfect life. I cannot let go of the past while still remembering what my family had lost. I fail to grasp the strength and courage of my grandmother and the meaning of *ganbatteru*—to claim you are OK so your loved ones can move on with their lives. Sometimes a greater love is to let go and continue to witness and reveal.

One of the workers vividly recalls when he was first hired at this facility. Shizuko greeted him with a nudge, almost a push, then a giggle. He was young; this was his first full-time job. Over a decade later, he remembers that first day. He and Shizuko matured and aged together.

I missed that history. A part of me regrets never knowing this aunt and one more family bond, one more opportunity to connect with the past. Yet these caregivers' stories help make Shizuko visible and connect me to a web of guarded memories. She lived a life of inclusion and participation, aided by those around her who gave meaning. I am privileged to witness the unseen, a past that had been concealed and now unfolds before me and I can share with the world.

I had begun my research into Shizuko's life trying to piece together a tragic story of disease, shame, abandonment, and loss. I thought the "system" would be at fault: a disabled person thrown away and left to die behind the walls, in the caverns of the antiquated mental health structure. There were challenging and dark moments while institutionalized, but Shizuko had survived. The very system that is often portrayed as heinous and uncaring proved me wrong. The system of care managed to nurture, tend for, and raise a young twenty-year-old woman with a disability who lived into her nineties. We found a home here.

"They" are not the villain nor at fault. "They" are not evil. "They" are caregivers who saved her life. "They" fulfilled the original pledge to take care of her. "They" affirm a belief in the good of people.

Shizuko's caregivers manifest an invisible army of philanthropists. They give to help beyond their job descriptions. They assist in ways obscured and hidden. They radically support a system of caring by working in the heart of darkness, a clandestine and too often concealed universe of the people with disabilities and elderly. They nourish a power of the human spirit to thrive in difficult situations. The poor are assigned to care for others in need. The poor, who give the most, dedicate themselves to the care for the poor. People of color labor in a system that often penalizes people of color, yet they journey onward. Those who struggle in their own private worlds pledge to support others as family, friends, and neighbors. Their spirit of empathy and engagement shatters the image of the altruist who often gives only to recreate an order in their own image; they look away and ignore those truly in need. Existing systems would crumble if it were not for the work of caregivers. The compassion I witness brutally exposes the world that envelopes my family and the history we cannot escape and yet continues to define us.

Courage to change by accepting
what can't be changed.
Shikata ga nai. It can't be helped.

I recall the phrase spoken
when Shizuko and my family were separated:
"*Yakusoku o mamoru*"—the vow to "*protect the promise.*"

PART EIGHT

BELONGING

29

Farming as a Radical Act

Shizuko could have been a great farmer. She is tough and determined. She under-
stands and adopts an ethic of hard work. She could pivot and adjust to changes
nature hurls upon her. She seems to accept fate. She carries a sorcerer's power: she
refuses to believe anything is wrong with her.

Throughout our family history, farmlands made life visible. We could feel life
all around us while working with nature and human nature. You can't hide
failures on a farm; neighbors see your work on display. We grow food for public
consumption. Judgment transpires as we internalize a bad weather year, poor
market prices, and a familiar reckoning of the harsh challenges of surviving
and trying to make a living. A farm transforms into a magical space because
it's openly ordinary—an exposing and revealing exploration into the soul of an
individual, a family, a community.

In 1976, I came back to the farm confused and broken. Years before, I had
escaped college and politics to venture into Japan, hoping to find an identity.
But I never became fluent in Japanese. During one language class in Tokyo,
my *sensei*, or "teacher," drilled us students on pronunciation. One thirty-year-
old white man from Australia brought a heavy accent into the classroom. We
all grinned with his take on vowel sounds and a clear rebranding of linguistic
identity. When it was my turn, I thought I sounded spot on, trying to mimic
a native tongue.

"Hei, Masumoto-san," the sensei sighed and shook his head. He continued to
critique my accent, correcting the slightest intonation error and even my pauses.
After class I took a bold and very un-Japanese act to confront the sensei and
pondered if my language skills were that terrible.

He paused, thought for a moment, then casually said, "When I see your face, Masumoto-san, I see Japanese. I expect perfection." I left realizing I could never be Japanese.

I returned for my final year at UC Berkeley and thought I could find a home in an academic and intellectual world. I had not prepared for the culture shock after spending two years overseas. I struggled in my sociology classes. I couldn't handle the theoretical frameworks and instead often gravitated to the everyday and authentic in my papers. For example, in a sociology of religion class taught by a well-known scholar, I wrote about the changing altar at the Fresno Buddhist Church and how symbols can change for a centuries-old religion and who makes those decisions at the local level . . . or not.

Besides, I also struggled because my heart had been broken from a bad relationship at that time, and I began to write bad poetry, like the lyrics of a bad country song with phrases like, "you stomped on my ticker" or "you crushed my love and done took my dreams" or "when you leave, don't let the screen door slam shut."

Dare I return to the farm I had once rejected? What life partner would want to work the earth and get their hands dirty? Almost all the Sansei I grew up with had left their family farms. They fled the dirt and so-called "backwards" valley. The bold departed. It seemed like only us "losers" were left behind. I came home defeated.

Back on the farm, I spent hours and hours working side by side with my father. He was a very reserved and quiet man. He shared only a few precious stories. For the entire first year home, I never missed a breakfast or lunch with him. My mother had taken a job off the farm to help support our finances, so my father and I cooked bad lunches together every day. He had leftovers, often *okazu*, which was our catchphrase for an assortment of vegetables with some meat all stir fried and mixed together. I opened canned soups and stews and warmed slices of Spam with yesterday's rice. We were isolated, alone and content. The farm was a place for me to hide, not to be seen. I returned to the ordinary.

Throughout her life, Shizuko takes walks and strolls, even in her wheelchair. I watch her cruise down the corridors of her facility. She is my guide as I trail after her, pausing to witness her interactions with others. The staff shares stories of her wandering and exploring nature. "Always on the move," they relate.

I can picture her as a child, as an adult, as an old woman, walking through our orchards in the spring. The brilliant peach and nectarine blossoms bathe her in delicate hues and tones. She is enveloped by the moment, soaring with the colors of life blooming. After a few weeks, the flowers complete their task; tiny fruit will be set and await harvest months later. The pink petals will float to the ground, dancing a final dance of impermanence as they flutter and drift to the earth. Shizuko lays on the earth, accepting the falling petals and leaves as they scatter and float home.

My mother shares a story of Shizuko meandering through the Japanese garden their father had created before the war. I had interpreted Shizuko's treks as her searching for something, perhaps to step back into Japan. Now I think differently. She journeys out of the shadows to special places: not to hide but to be welcomed. I'm wrong to imagine her in a Japan that she never knew. It's not about a destination or end. She seeks shelter in the open air of a garden. Shizuko searches in her mind to engage.

The farm became a refuge for me. I would have many moments to reflect alone, but I was also surrounded by stories from my family and neighbors. That's why oral histories and authentic voices mattered. Wave after wave of immigrants had carved new lives here in our valley. They continued to come to work the land and forge new beginnings all the while carrying their historical baggage. The land fosters a place to recover for war veterans seeking an asylum from trauma. The natural world of farming can transform into a sanctuary to escape the lies of exploitation, racism, and class segregation.

Yet farmers are too often discounted and made invisible. People ignore the axiom that food connects with life and life connects with food.

As I aged, I have ascertained how farms acclimate into places of healing. The people here stay put and learn to live with neighbors. The phrase that fences make for good neighbors does ring with some truth, so long as we don't live in isolation. Silence lives in these lands, it's part of the everyday work rhythms. Yet stories float in the air, ripe for picking but only if you ask.

I have come to appreciate things old. A Japanese zen aesthetics term, often used when describing a zen garden, is *koko*, which translates into "weathered" and "basic" —to value things that are simple and with restraint—they can symbolize a clarity and wisdom gained over time. Life can be better with age. A farmer has the potential to grow old and wise, an atonement within.

> *Shizuko and I are late bloomers. We discover each other in the pursuit of uncovering a revelation: we farm secrets. For the Issei, these farmlands were sites where mysteries were kept. For the Nisei, these were venues where the contradictions of life could be safe. For Sansei, here the unspoken could be explored. Like the mystery of Shizuko.*
>
> *Our farm carries a camouflaged history. Deep in our piece of the earth, buried are harsh realities of Alien Land Laws and relocation. Today, a new interest in food reveals a new understanding of where food comes from and the hands that feed you. These realities are no longer hidden and transform into a social and spiritual fabric capturing the context of growing food.*
>
> *I walk in Shizuko's footprints. Her movements embody a magical quest: being lost is ordinary. Her searching exemplifies acts of defiance, seeking the undefined places where ghosts inhabit in our lives.*
>
> *With meningitis, she seemed to have survived as a child who never grew, which can sound judgmental and condescending. Yet there's something wickedly intriguing about that: keeping an innocence for the rest of your life, surviving with selective and imaginary memories. She symbolizes those who accept the role of power and powerlessness in our world. No different than a good farmer when confronted by the forces of nature.*

I farm a sense of history. After decades working this land, I've come to terms when natural forces result in a defect or when market forces define and label a bad peach. Systems and institutions in the food world create standards, industrial standards not always aligned with nature. We're obligated to work and live within these systems: big fruit is defined as better, a redder peach or nectarine more attractive, shelf life valued over taste.

Or not. Our farm has thrived by incorporating a human element into our definition of what's right. Taste matters not just appearances. Success comes in all sizes. The color of skin has no bearing on what's inside. All these symbiotic relationships combine for something wonderful. The ultimate goal drives us to find a home for so-called "ugly" fruit. We have come to trust our own stories. We must remember to create authentic flavors and life. Emotions matter, not just the facts of sales figures.

I can touch and feel history in our fields. Vines on "the hill" (a slightly higher section of the farm, only a few feet above the rest of the fields—but when I irrigate, I quickly learned that water does not flow uphill) were planted the year my grandfather had a heart attack and died in 1952, before I was born. I planted a block of three hundred peach trees with my father in 1968 as a restless teenager who couldn't wait to flee the seemingly empty lands around me. Our "young" vineyard was planted in 1981, a small two-acre block, where I first introduced my wife-to-be, Marcy, to my father. She grew up on a goat dairy in Southern California and her farming lineage was embedded in Wisconsin German Lutheran and Catholic stock, a very different history than my family, but her agrarian roots bonded with our family farm. You could say the earth connected us as we blended two diverse yet common genealogies and traditions. She was planting vine runners with mud on her hands and dirt on her face. She looked up and saw his silhouette and a smile on his face.

History revolves around both nature and human nature on our farm. Actions have meaning, characters engage and withdraw, settings provide the stage and backdrop for drama. Who writes this history? We constantly choose what to remember and forget.

I came home to farm memories. This land evolves from geologic epochs with timelines that dwarf my small presence here. From earliest creation of landforms and water to the asteroid destruction and rebirth of life on the planet, followed by historic periods of ice ages and the continental drift, our farmland was twisted and recast, molded and reshaped into a fragile piece of earth my family now borrows. This valley was once an ancient lakebed. Left behind are rich aquifers blessing us with life-giving ground water. As time passed, a natural partnership was founded—the towering Sierras captured winter snowpacks which every spring and summer channeled into raging rivers feeding a newly dry and arid lowland.

Earth memory lives in our soils. Sandy loam silt created by massive evolutionary forces of nature dominate this part of the valley I farm. We've been farming organically since the 1980s; organic matter and microbial life now churn beneath the surface, a living soil biology that hums with life.

In more recent times, nature has left vivid reminders of its power and presence. I can distinctly remember rains on raisins the year I came back to the farm after college in 1976 and then déjà vu in 1978. Entire crops were destroyed; I watched my father painfully disking the rotting grapes back into the earth, a year's worth of labor buried in the dirt and dust. A late spring frost in the early 1980s burned delicate, pale green grape shoots just as they were emerging from dormancy. For weeks, the patches of brown, lifeless decay scarred our vineyards. I could map out the lowest sections of our land where a seemingly gentle decline in the terrain allowed the killing freeze to pool and settle. Currently, every summer with climate change, heat waves last longer, and we try to decipher the impact on fruit ripening, sometimes racing to pick before peaches melt in the heat. In the end, we understand we cannot control nature and learn to accept. Accessibility to what nature gives us has become our mantra.

Yet human nature prejudices my thinking. I recall good and bad harvests based primarily on prices and rejections. I was stunned during the summer of 1985 when peach prices collapsed, and we sold fruit at a nickel a pound. I felt like we were living amid the Great Depression when our family struggled like the rest of the nation and world. My gloom was momentarily interrupted when I wrote an article for the *LA Times* entitled "Epitaph for a Peach" and the column was syndicated across the nation. I received dozens of letters encouraging me to keep something worth saving. Then one voice sounded like a note of support but instead the writer asked, "And where can I buy your peaches for a nickel a pound?"

I too easily push the ancestors away from the land, believing that the past is the past and never understanding the whole. Emotions do matter—like family histories and ties that bind. Solely dollars lost or gained do not define our farm. We seek not success but significance, a circular process of integration and disintegration.

I imagine the ancient footprints of the Gashowu, or Casson Yokuts—natives who walked this land. In the evening, I stand outside, listening to the sound of irrigation water bringing life to the vines and orchards. I look up and wonder who else occupied this land? Were the Casson Yokuts, farmers? Or was this land part of a late autumn trail taken as a people journeyed from summer homes in the hills and mountains to the winter in flatlands by rivers and streams?

I look at a map of the Kings River, which races down from the Sierras into the valley. There's a major bend in the river due east from our farm. I believe that in wet and snowy years the river overflowed its banks and flooded our region, contributing to a shift in the underground aquifers hundreds and hundreds of years ago.

When we re-drilled a new well for our farm in 2001, I located the original well drilling company that had done the work seventy years before. It was protocol to make a well log of the many layers of earth the drill bore through. In the records, I could read where they hit silt then a sandy layer with some rocky stones and occasional hardpan. In one line they listed "redwood pieces" some thirty feet below the surface, just as they hit the first groundwater table line. Our valley floor did not host redwood trees, even in ancient times. The well driller casually mentioned that such discoveries were not that unusual. He summarized that redwood was a common indicator of the nearby river flooding the region with debris drifting down from the mountains and embedding itself in a layer of time.

The Casson Yokuts may have walked the new trails of a temporary bank on our farm during a flood. They may have spent a winter here, chilled by our night temperatures in the '30s but rarely snow or freezes. A shroud of fog prevents temperatures from dipping low, rabbit-skin blankets and a fire could make life bearable. But on a clear night they could look up and witness a universe of stars and the moon dancing across the sky.

Gashowu. Casson. These were their tribal names. I have come to learn that Yokut is an exonym, a name invented by English speaking settlers and historians. Who has the right to name a people and their history? Were the names Gashowu and Casson kept under wraps, hidden from the world until reclaimed by descendants?

These ghosts inhabit the soil I farm while I foolishly believe I was the only one who wandered across this tiny piece of ground. Some accounts describe the natives eating acorns and who were seed gatherers and hunters. Not farmers. But they too lived off this land.

My family now joins this history. My grandparents were not compelled to return to their homeland Japan even though their adopted country, America, lied and incarcerated them and their family. Instead, they came back here to farm. The land meant survival, nurturing food from the earth, meaning revealed from a place my family now calls home. I honor all these memories of ghosts, along with the others who preceded and followed. Gashowu. Casson. Mexicans. Blacks. Chinese. Japanese. Armenians. Italians. Portuguese, specifically from the Azores. German Mennonites. Swedes. Later a new wave. Filipinos. Sikhs. Iranians. Central Americans. Russian Armenians. Pacific Islanders. Native Hawaiians. Asian Indians. Laotians. Cambodians. The Hmong. And many others I'm sure I missed.

They live as obscure chapters from the past right in front of me. Not revealed. Part of the mystery to be lived. To make history by learning history.

Shizuko finds a place on this farm. Here, we farm the old. One row of vines was planted in 1918. That was the year my Baachan Masumoto arrived from Japan to meet her husband (he had immigrated in the late 1890s). The Sugimoto family had arrived as part of this early wave of Japanese immigrants in the early 1900s. A year after these vines were planted, Shizuko was born. In front of our farmhouse another two-acre block of over one thousand vines that were planted in 1923. Shizuko would contract meningitis two years later when the vines bore their first crop.

A Japanese family, Thos S. Murakami, once owned this property in the 1913. Later, a part of the farm was obtained by the I. Matsuo family in 1920. I am unable to discover more information other than the plat map of Fresno County, which shows our tract of land with a name, surrounded by names of my neighbors. How did these families circumvent the Alien Land Laws preventing "Orientals" from land ownership? I know of a few families who purchased land in the name of their American-born infant children—was Thos one of these names? Most families, though, struggled to make land payments and a few survived as landowners. The

Murakami and the Matsuo families were only recorded once. A few years later another plat map was created, and their names were replaced by another family.

Both the Masumotos and Sugimotos were farmworkers. They sometimes worked as part of a migrant Japanese labor crew, a group of workers arriving at one farm to prune or pick for a few days, then moving to another farm and another. It's possible my Grandmother Sugimoto worked the vines in front of our house while she carried Shizuko. Or perhaps after meningitis, Shizuko wandered and played in these fields while her parents toiled. Labor crews often return to the same vineyard year after year, a new owner inheriting a workforce who know the lay of the land. Shizuko may have grown up here, a few feet from our front door. These imaginations become my resident memories of a sacred space. A place where Shizuko belongs and her disabilities blend in.

Family memories thrive in this fertile soil. We wear scars from this history; typically they heal and are not deep wounds from which we will never recover. For others, the burden may have been too great; those families eventually left these lands, driven away by the hard physical work, inconsistencies of nature, and brutal financial realities of the low prices for foods they grew. Or they found better livelihoods. My family stayed. Occasionally I hear a story, reminding me of the literal scars we still wear.

At the funeral of an uncle, a story was shared, part of the eulogy of memories. We talked of my late uncle working as a teenager, picking grapes for raisins with his siblings. One brother then casually mentioned the scar on the corner of his mouth where the two dangerously amused themselves at the end of a work day. After a day of picking grapes for raisins, the two boys began racing back to the car for the drive home. They each held a grape knife in their right hand; the uniquely shaped blade was curved and not straight, designed to hook the stalk or peduncle of a cluster of grapes and easily and cleanly slice off the bunch from the vine cane.

One brother raced in front of the other. The younger one ran alongside, to the left. I paused, envisioning my late uncle laughing as he dashed ahead. But the image was incomplete, my other uncle pointed to the right corner of his mouth where the blade sliced his flesh. I queried, "Didn't you hold the knives in your right hand? So how could your right side of your lips get sliced, carved and slit?" Our family cringed with the image.

My uncle stood and shook his head. "You don't understand," he grumbled. Then he barked, "I fell behind but thought I could sprint past with a last push. So your uncle suddenly stopped, whipped around and yelled—'You shall not pass' and stuck out his arms with his knife extended."

Ouch. We could all visualize the moment, the act of two brothers "horsing around in a vineyard" that would bond them forever, even at a funeral.

Our bodies wear marks that brand a history into our flesh. A chipped tooth. Gash on a forehead. Smashed fingernail. Torn flesh on an arm or leg. Hernias from lifting too much. Torn knee cartilage from falling off ladders. A lump on the head from trying to catch a metal ball hitch thrown into the air—resulting in a concussion. Battle wounds we recalled from a childhood as we grew and remembering bodies that bled and whose blood stains the earth, distinguishing their presence. Triggers for stories we embody. Everyday trauma as ordinary.

Shizuko wants to feed herself. She does not eat alone though; food is a communal act for her. While growing up, my mom recalls Shizuko always playing with her food. Their mother was "very patient" with Shizuko. A bit of sarcasm slips into the story of my mother being afraid of Shizuko when they all shared a meal. "Shizuko liked to launch her food at me," my mom recalls. "She liked to aim at me . . . Why me?" My mom shakes her head ever so slightly. "Very patient . . ."

The staff has to make Shizuko's meals eatable, so they cut everything into small bites. She eats with the residents at a special table with proper distance from others. Of course, she flings her coffee cups when finished. If she doesn't approve of a food, she simply tosses it off her plate, a spontaneous expressive act of protest, a daily potion of life she delivers. Fortunately, the staff recalls, Shizuko liked ice cream, and that is not flung into the air.

I sometimes wish I had the courage to be so revealing.

"Sugi is the longest surviving client we ever had," they repeat. "We sometimes sought her out just to be with her, taking a break from the routine to replenish energy." A grin accompanies that statement and I'm sure there's more unspoken: words unsaid but without the weight of a dark poem. Shizuko teaches without teaching.

America wants to forget where their food comes from and the farmers' and farmworkers' hands. Waves of immigrants arrive at our shores to work this land. They are faceless and hidden in rural enclaves. America labels them aliens or illegals or undocumented. Color matters, from the color of the laborer's skin to the colors of their documents—a yellowed alien registration card, a green card bestowing them the chance to pick our produce—and the color of the border patrol, a dark olive-green work shirt with a green cap.

I remember as a kid in the 1960s, the pale green truck of immigration patrol would cruise through our country roads, searching for "illegals" to pick up and deport. I witnessed field workers panicking with the sight of that color seen through the branches and tree limbs. Some fled, running down the rows of a neighbor's orchard, hiding until the green vehicle departed and they could safely return to their ladders and buckets to resume harvesting food for America's dinner tables.

For most eaters, food magically appears at the grocery store and on their plates. The illusion extends to how food disappears, from food waste we ignore and pretend does not exist to the "ugly" produce that never makes it to market, a cosmetic flaw construed as a defect, an odd shape labeled as unwanted. Even the size of a peach or nectarine undergoes reassessment annually: what is small and undersized today was fine a decade ago. This cloak of judgment masquerades as a powerful defining force in our daily interactions. Others claim the authority to designate and sanction good versus bad, normal versus abnormal.

But a change has been brewing. You are what you eat—a growing conscious-ness of acceptance is altering the landscape of food and farming. The models of capitalism and forces idolizing efficiency and productivity are currently being reevaluated and rethought.

My quest to explore the unrevealed life surrounding Shizuko and to reexam-ine my definition of "what is normal" has exposed my beliefs of farming and our family. I don't want to forget. My family was not American by certain standards, yet we were at the heart of what is America and a quest for freedom and diversi-ty. And we grow food. We quickly forget that a hundred years ago, the majority of Americans lived in rural areas. The majority of people worked on farms and with food. Most of our family roots were grounded in the earth and dirt. Rural folks were "normal" back then and in the majority with the power to enable.

Technology and industrialization changed it all. Henry Ford's tractor began a revolution that displaced millions from the fields, and many would gladly escape the harsh physical labor of agriculture. I think of a quote allegedly attributed to Henry Ford who grew exasperated with the slowness of his invention being adopted. "Ask a farmer what he needs and he'll answer: I need a faster horse."

It took half a century, from the early 1900s when Ford first introduced his mechanical wonder to the 1950s when tractors had replaced horses on the majority of farms. A few decades later, by the 1970s, very few utilized horses or mules. I grew up never knowing how to hook up a plow to a horse, despite making use of our old red barn, which was designed with stalls and feeding doors that opened for animals. We tore down another huge structure that once housed a milking parlor, but the low beams often got in the way of our forklift mast when we tried to fit modern wood and metal bins into spots hay bales once were stacked. These changes compel us to forget and unremember.

Amnesia too often guided our thinking. We were taught that the old ways were antiquated and kept a farmer from growing and evolving. I recall my father growing weary and confused as agribusiness pushed our operation towards the use of more herbicides and pesticides to increase productivity. But as I transitioned to organic farming, suddenly his memories of weed control without chemicals became essential. We salvaged an old vineyard French plow from our junk pile, and he taught me how to use it, a mechanical weed control method few farmers utilize anymore. My father's native competency and indigenous knowledge were valued. He found a new significant role on a modern farm.

Shizuko and the disability community are part of the ordinary story of America and the drive to belong. Just as I never want America to forget what a great peach or nectarine tastes like, we must never forget the world of Shizuko and people with disabilities. Memories dictate how we define this brave new world where emotions and a sense of history count: just as our old heirloom peaches belong in the world of food, Shizuko belongs in our family tree along with our family secrets. The story behind these secrets matters: they are part of the context of a sweet fruit and family

history. Shizuko's magical story is part of our family farm because she's family and
can't be separated.

   Organic farming seeks to build and foster biodiversity on the land, in the plants,
and in the soil. We also strive to forge a livelihood that values human diversity for
all, not only race, religion, and culture, but also all capacities and conditions. We
believe in diversity in all of nature to the fullest.

Farming has the power to build and maintain authentic relationships. Like good neighbors who stay with the land and the history of a place. We had one neighbor, Kamm Oliver, a kind man "with a good heart" as my mom and dad shared. I didn't completely understand that characterization until I interviewed him as part of an oral history project of Japanese American farmers. He was a good neighbor to a nearby Japanese American farm family, the Hiyamas. When the Hiyamas were evacuated to and imprisoned in the Arizona desert, the Oliver family managed their farm and sent them any profits. Later, Kamm loaded his truck with the help of another farmer neighbor, the Feavers. They drove from Central California to Gila River Relocation Center in Arizona, a round trip trek of over 1,200 miles. He journeyed through the desert and delivered some furniture and household goods to his neighbor. "I drove through the parched lands . . . I could not believe our government would lock up people in such a godforsaken place." Kamm shared with me.

   Family farming epitomizes interdependence. We work with nature, striving not to dominate nor control. We team with other field workers and suppliers who provide essential resources to repair, replenish, and flourish. We only thrive with the right partners. Brokers and sellers assist in distribution. Shippers and drivers take care of our fruits in transit. And then the final hands distribute and market our produce to restaurants, grocers, farmers' markets, and food service. We can all thrive as good neighbors.

   Shizuko can teach me much about interdependence. Her life depends on others but she in turn gives meaning and significance to her caregivers and partners. Her team of supporters unify and collaborate in her care: they embody the spirit of a whole life. Shizuko is and was never alone. She now completes us—our family is more with her.

Mysteries enrich our soil; stories empower our family. The simple act of coming home, farming organically, living with nature—perhaps these are the ultimate acts of resistance and protest. Deeds of defiance and resilience, embodied in Shizuko and her coming home to family. Shizuko gives us memories, the medicine for a healthy family transformation and the ties that bind us to a piece of earth called a family farm. History undenied: to remember becomes a radical act. Acceptance first. Then we struggle and will fight to discover where we belong.

> *I believe Shizuko would have been a great farmer. There's an adage circulating in the farm community. I heard it after a hailstorm destroyed a block of our peaches just days before harvest. I watched the cold dark clouds march across our valley, the thunder and lightning first pounding our farm, then a neighbor's fields and then another, hail pummeling fruits, knocking them to the ground, slicing the delicate skin, slashing the flesh with juices oozing out. The rot will soon fester. I stood outside witnessing the unfolding trauma. A neighbor contacted me and a silence bonded two farmers.*
>
> *Then he softly spoke: "They did an autopsy on some old farmers. And when they opened them up, the found they were all filled with 'next years.'"*
>
> *Shizuko is filled with next years.*

30

Passing with Tennis Shoes and Blinking Lights

Shizuko "Sugi" Sugimoto

Born October 13, 1919
Died August 1, 2013

She lives almost to her ninety-fourth birthday. She is the oldest client in the system at the Central Valley Regional Center, whose mission is to help individuals with developmental disabilities to reach their goals. She has spent over seventy years institutionalized.

The commitment to take care of her was fulfilled. From a hot August day in 1942
until her death in August of 2013, the promise made was fulfilled. After decades of
care, the original vow was passed along, and a pledge amazingly achieved.
   And Shizuko survived to tell her story on her own terms.

August 10, 2013

At the memorial service for Shizuko, family and caregivers gathered. Stories were shared.

My aunt told how Shizuko loved taking an *ofuro*, or a Japanese bath. On our farm, we have a vestige *ofuro* that was made from sheet metal molded into a rectangular box. In the past, one by one, family members cleaned up after a long day in the fields. They washed up outside the tub, the steam rising to cleanse and open pores. Then they paused for a moment from their aches and pains and slipped into a tub of soothing hot water. The liquid was often heated by a small fire beneath it. Each family member took turns stoking the flames with wood and everyone shared the same communal water.

"And Shizuko loved holding hands," my aunt remembered. "She held hands with all of us, with brothers, sisters, and especially Mom."

An uncle recalled Shizuko being a handful. He remembered when they had to put her in the hospital "when everyone went to camp."

My mom confessed it was a challenge to live with Shizuko at times. Then she joked about how Shizuko loved to throw things. "Even at us!" she added.

Staff members from the assisted care facility honored Shizuko with their presence. They added stories of her energy and spirit. Shizuko laughed all the time. "She didn't understand that anything was wrong with her, so she ran all over the place."

Once when she broke her arm and needed to wear a cast, she would not slow down. "She kept trying to get the cast off. In fact, she pounded on it to crack it open and eventually we had to remove it early. Shizuko was like that. Even when she got sick, she just kept coming back strong and fighting."

They considered it a blessing to work with her.

A hospice nurse thought that "finding family and regular visitors changed Shizuko. It helped her last so much longer."

Another caregiver, who knew Shizuko for the longest, had always wondered about Shizuko's family. She was pleased to see the reunion and the importance of family stories, part of Shizuko returning to the ordinary world. She commented, "Families are more mixed, spread out, and it's harder to remember family history. Rainbow families need stories more than ever."

Even on her final day, the nurse said that Shizuko was still up and about and had just laid down to nap when she passed. "So right up to the end, she was active and picked her own time. She always did what she wanted."

The caregivers told story after story, each with more vivid and lively details as they reminisced about the life of a patient they truly loved. Her caregivers created a world of optimism as if Shizuko could have a choice about her destiny. They offered an atonement, a reparation given to Shizuko for a hard life lived. As the tales were shared, many of the family, including myself, began to slump our shoulders and drop our heads, staring at the floor.

I then added a story I had heard of Shizuko's love for morning coffee. As a final gesture, we passed out empty plastic cups and pretended to take a sip of the morning brew. Then one by one, like a final salute, we mimicked Shizuko's character by tossing the cups blindly behind us. A carefree spirit of defiance.

Of course, many of the family members did not reenact the scene completely and I forgive them for not participating. Most peeked behind them before they tossed their cups, not wanting to hit anyone, seeking to avoid direct contact. But Shizuko never looked back; she was liberated from such details. If only we too could witness disability and be liberated.

I don't have the language to explain Shizuko's plight. I am aware of some of her challenges and sufferings, but a silence must fill the gaps. Similar to my family's internment and imprisonment, I have sketches and a few stories—but I was born into a muted world and grew up without reference points, without a deeper understanding of what happened.

I have two memories: those that must be documented and recorded and those that are silent. I grew up in a family and community that taught me to remember and forget. Shizuko's tragic yet dramatic story begins with her meningitis. She was not alone. Tens of thousands were affected, families scarred, lives forever altered. Yet there is no collective memory, no memorials to those who died, no historical markers in our minds of such diseases that created numerous disabilities. Those with intellectual disorders remain in the shadows. Perhaps because it's too personal, seemingly invisible, without heroic cures, no simple narrative with a beginning, middle, and climatic end.

While more and more of the public is learning about the imprisonment of Japanese Americans during World War II, it remains part of a hidden history, a black spot in our past in a nation that believes in freedom and rights. For my family, to remember becomes a radical act. Creating a memory culture will transform lives. My call is to wade through the toxic sludge of history and tell the story to the world. Yet I live with the fear no one will listen.

Only when the threads of my family history are woven together can the interdependence of life be conceived as flashes, each story a spark that leads to another and another truth. Now I understand the challenge to look for the blinking lights and solicit the ghosts to respond, knowing they rarely respond. Growing up, my father shared a phrase that manifested his philosophy of life: *Nana korobi ya oki*, or "Fall down seven times, get up eight." It was the wisdom of a farmer who accepted the winds of nature. It was the strategy to cope with our family's struggles: to endure with tolerance. My quiet and reserved father shared his simple advice about acceptance—and how I could construct my own identity.

It takes strength to remember and to forget. This is what I have inherited.

At Shizuko's memorial service, on a makeshift altar, I place a box of her prized processions: her shoes. They are all children's tennis shoes, a kid's size 2 that fit her tiny feet. Some are tattered and worn from the running and scooting she did on a daily basis. She loved the fancy colors and glitter on many of the pairs.

One pair stands out: the one with flashing lights. She loved the modern shoes with a series of embedded and colorful bulbs that would switch on with each step. She'd stomp around and watch them ignite, grinning with every stride and burst, her path thereupon illuminated. These are her favorite shoes; they sparkle brightly and Shizuko's spirit shines boldly.

Though in the morning we may have radiant health,
in the evening we may return to white ashes.
When the winds of impermanence blow . . .
      from Buddhist funeral ritual

31

Farm Walks

Shizuko can walk freely now. She can roam the halls, amble through the fields, trek over the countryside. As a child, she traversed the farms where her family labored, finding comfort in the solitude, in the silent orchards and vineyards. She can revisit ordinary places that shaped her life.

With her walks Shizuko finds the agency to live. She masters her limitations and seeks joy in people around her. She learns how to shape a part of her own life. She remains an original, unique to herself, with her own story. A positive narrative not incumbered by disabilities while fully aware of the realities. She forgets everything and remembers everything. This is to be awake.

She allows us to accompany her. I can return to the world with Shizuko at my side: she is remembered and reclaimed. A life without regret nor shame. Deliberate. Persistent. With tranquility. She can now be with family.

Baachan Masumoto left her footprints on our farm, walking fields she never owned but discovering a place she came to call home. Even in her final years at our home when she was in her eighties, she'd take long walks, meandering down our avenues and past the orchards and vineyards. I'd ask her where she was walking. She explained, "Through the rice fields. I'm walking home." The memories always returned. I knew exactly those paddies and the narrow embankments that divided the plots, the same ones I once walked during my years studying in Japan as a twenty-year-old when I journeyed to her native village outside of Kumamoto. Baachan Masumoto seemed content, walking for hours as she grafted memories of the past onto the present.

Sometimes I walked with her in silence. She would hum a Japanese children's folk song. I'd ask: "What song are you singing?"

Her response was: "Sing? I don't know how to sing . . ."

I thought of a moment in Japan when I was with friends on a train station platform. Three children were playing and singing a song, a child's game I did not recognize. "*Nira meko shimasho!*"

I asked my friends what that meant. They giggled then answered, it was a child's teasing game about trying to make each other laugh. "Every Japanese knows that game," my friend answered. I didn't. I again realized I could never be Japanese. I discovered why many Sansei were afraid to go to Japan.

I walked with my Baachan through familiar fields. Once, she stopped, stepped behind a grapevine and pulled down her pants and squatted to pee. She quickly finished, stood up, and continued the walk. She was at home, a familiar place in her mind: safe, free, and secure.

After my father's stroke in his late seventies, he relearned how to walk and work these peaches and grapes. He found joy in pruning, slowly working each tree and vine, believing that if you pruned a branch in winter, you were destined to see it through to summer harvest and one more year. I farm organically, feeding the soil and building life, an abundance of microorganisms thrives in this earth celebrating the diversity required for a healthy system to work at a high level. This is the place I will spend the rest of my life and one day too come to rest here: I have found home.

Our daughter, Nikiko, fourth-generation Japanese American, now walks this road back. She is full of energy, optimism, and passion. She will redefine the meaning of this family farm and the history she has inherited. She not only supports but now partners with newfound hopes and dreams that give life. Her younger brother, Korio, teams with his sister to carve out a new and different identity in these fields. The two siblings walk the same trails as generations before but with a different rhythm and cadence. Our shared story of change and transition will continue to unfold and grow.

We have fifty-year-old peach trees, a wonderful heirloom variety called Sun Crest. I helped plant these trees with my father in 1968. You can still see the ones I dug a hole for and set the tree in—they are not as straight and upright as those my father worked. My trees lean slightly to one side and are not exactly even with the others in their rows, the mark of an impatient teenage boy that I have had to live and work with for decades. Nikiko inherits my crooked trees.

Occasionally, a few trees in this block of three hundred begin to die. Branches wither, fruit falls off in the spring, limbs crack and grow limp. We saw them down, an act of euthanasia as we tend to the elderly. The majority of the orchard thrives, fifty years for a commercial operation is unheard of, most fields last about ten to fifteen years before production falls and a new variety that's redder and bigger with longer shelf life overshadows the old. This orchard stands for what we believe in—flavor, taste, quality, respect for the past, honoring the history of life.

When I do remove an old tree, I saw the trunk and inspect the tree rings to see and feel history. The early circles grew wide and fat, denoting rapid growth and good farm years for my family. Thousands of Japanese American family farms, following the war years, were able to plant themselves and carve a place where they settled and no longer were identified as sojourners. To be American is to belong.

I can point to the ring when I left the farm for college, believing I'd never return. I can see when Shizuko returned to this region, coming back to nearby group homes we drove past for decades, unaware of her presence. My fingers walk across the surface of the trunk—this was when Marcy, my wife, settled on the farm, Nikiko and then Korio were born, and when my father passed. Rings mark the year I had triple bypass heart surgery when my cardiologist said I probably already had a heart attack but was saved by farm work over the decades which enabled collateral arteries around my heart to slowly grow and gradually compensate for the blockage. The recent rings demark Nikiko's reign on this farm and her beginning. Along the edge, the narrow bands of drought years on our farm coincide with the moment Shizuko discovered us. This is where she resides.

The one-hundred-year-old grapevines in front of our farmhouse embody the timeline of Shizuko. Her ghost is embedded in their history, along with all the ghosts who reunite with the world of nature alive on this farm and the human nature of the people who once walked this earth. The ghosts silently announce their presence with every new season—buds push anew each spring, leaves flourish in the summer heat, and grapes grow fat and sweet by autumn. They then sleep each winter, allowing time to regenerate and whisper: remember. I hope they will stay and soar once more and once more. Only then can I fully grasp the context of history and time that creates meaning and understanding, linking me with the past in the present and a voice to explore the future.

I visualize walking these grounds with Shizuko. The slow pace of a stroll, the act of placing one foot in front of the other, the sound of earth crunching beneath our soles. This physicality bridges thoughts from the linear and logical to the holistic and imaginative. The spirit of my history remains alive as I walk this land. I have come to learn of Shizuko's story that is filled with a contagious spirit. Her ghost is no longer incomplete. I can't stop the past winds of change that separated her from family. Yet if I keep my eyes open, I can see in the twisted and gnarled vine trunk's life that pauses for a moment. Time enough to tell her story, to be awake and feel. We can't stay like this for long, but I can have her next to me today. A final walk offering freedom to find wisdom.

The breezes swirl around these fields. A light coat of dirt blankets all surfaces. Each of my steps kicks up a small cloud of dust; the particles float and drift in the air, the moment eternal until they gently fall back to the earth, returning home. I envision the billows of dust Shizuko would have created with each of her shuffling footsteps. I could follow her trek from a distance, simply tracing the puffs as they meandered down a farm trail and cut through an open field along a footpath, sharing the route with small wild farm creatures and those who traversed this land before her.

I follow their path, the spirit of family, history and secrets surround me. I call out the names of those no longer with us on earth: my Baachans, my Jiichans, my father, my mother, my sister, my uncles, aunts, and cousins. Shizuko. No one hears and everyone hears. Their ghosts return to shelter me, announcing their presence as survivors. I can carry on because we have each other. Remember all the love and the history we share at this moment, to be awake and feel together. To struggle, to journey beyond acceptance. To leave a legacy of belonging. Like "natural grasses" on a family farm.

We have shaped our histories from the hands we were dealt. We reclaim parts of ourselves that had been lost. We redeem actions as well as regrets that complete our stories. Memories are recast and reshaped without remorse. To remember the future and reimagine the past. To accept the love from others and grant ourselves forgiveness and closure.

The ghosts need to know.
The ghosts whisper: "Just listen."

We will remember.
To finally belong.
Shikata ga nai.
It can't be helped.

The Wall and the Bench

Autumn 2013

The cast bronze plaque has Shizuko's name, birth and death dates in gold. The four-by-four-inch square has small holes drilled in the back but not all the way through: just enough to be mounted on the wall at the Japanese American mausoleum at the Mountain View Cemetery. Her ashes lie just below sister Akiko, near brother Shigeru and near her mother and father. She will finally be united with family and the place she belongs.

Call it destiny, but I screw up. I order the wrong type of plaque. It is four-by-four, bronze with gold lettering, but I didn't realize all the other Sugimoto plaques also included an ornamental leaf border. The one I hold is plain and simple, ordinary without the decorative garnishing. For a moment, I think it appropriate to include Shizuko with a different plaque. Fitting to be cast as a misfit.

But this is her final resting place, to match and be alongside siblings and father and mother, to be part of the family. I order a recast name plate with the ornamental trim and have it remounted. She finally fits and can rest. I keep the wrong one as my personal memorial.

How will I remember Shizuko?

Every winter, I think of the power of nature as I continue to practice the annual rite of pruning organic peach, nectarine, and apricot trees. The art of snipping and cutting, the clearing and removal of stems and branches with the goal of allowing sunlight to penetrate the canopy. In the cold of winter, you try to envision the summer sunlight warming the ripening fruit. Once you master this art of recognizing negative space, you can feel the power of options, choices, and actions that generate confidence that you can see the future in the present.

On our farm, thousands of seeds are planted each season as we allow native grasses to fill the ecosystem of an organic farm. The lush green growth of spring flourishes as plants flower and bloom, then in the dry summer heat they wither and dry, dropping seeds for the next year and the next. It's a cycle of birth and death, replenishing the earth with seeds of hope and a spirit of renewal.

As a writer, I make myself available for stories. Some will remain incomplete. I will never know all the facts. This is part of authenticity. That's why I'm intrigued by creative nonfiction: I honor people and their past by not altering details and historical realities. I don't have the skills of a fiction writer to probe, explore, and escape into the world with a novelist's imagination. Instead, the contradictions and gaps in life survive as both wounds and scar tissue and attract my curiosity and attention. The act of collecting the words that bind us as a family, as a community, still matter. Context counts. That's how the ghosts of life work; and if I'm lucky, I can find the places I belong. I can now envision myself as an actor and participant in family legacies. In the end, all we have are stories with memories.

At the Fresno Fairgrounds, I dedicate a simple bench to Shizuko. A basic cement slab is mounted on thick cement legs and placed near the monument for the Japanese American Assembly Center. The area is in a busy corridor near the Chance Avenue entrance booth and in front of the commerce building where thousands visit. The bench allows numerous fair visitors a place to pause and relax while watching the steady wave of fairgoers pass by.

I sit and watch families and groups stream past. The excitement of being at the fair brings smiles and energy to the crowds. They journey into the exhibits and cross into the carnival area. They stop at food booths and slip into the racetrack to "bet on the ponies." They reach out to embrace, squeeze, or pinch one another as if to proclaim, "You've got a friend," just as Shizuko did in her own way.

Their stories flow past me and leave me behind as I rest on Shizuko's simple bench. I think of the past and present, the history in all our lives. But like my family and Shizuko, I will too move on.

A plaque mounted on the bench side reads:

> In memory of Shizuko "Sugi" Sugimoto (1919–2013)
> Honoring those with disabilities and special needs
> who were separated from their families
> during the World War II Relocation and Internment
> of Japanese Americans from the West Coast.
> We remain inspired by their resilience.

To finally belong.
Shikata ga nai.
It can't be helped.

ILLUSTRATOR NOTES

Patricia Wakida

About the Artwork:

From the age of seven to seventeen, I grew up across the street from an active winery. On winter mornings, fog so white and wooly that we couldn't see the tank cars resting on the train tracks just across the way would descend, and "foggy day schedules," where the public schools opened late, were a real thing. Our neighborhood bore the scent of orange blossoms and rich earth mixed with a distinctive tang of fermented grapes. My American-born grandparents on both sides were farmers before the war, working the grapevines, plum orchards, or tomato fields. Even as kids, relatives who still farmed would invite us to pick leftover fruits once the harvest season was officially over. This is how I learned that grape leaves are itchy and required long sleeves for handling and that horned toads sometimes hid in the shade of the vines. I knew that temperatures dropping in the dead of winter might mean that the citrus farmers would have to run night floodlights and gigantic fans between rows of oranges to save the crop from a freeze, or that heavy rain in early spring when the blossoms were still yearning for pollination and a hailstorm on an orchard pre-harvest could destroy an entire year's work.

In January 2018, Mas approached me with a draft of the book you are holding in your hands and asked if I would be interested in illustrating a deeply personal, family story about an unusual case of family separation and community shame. I was intrigued. The manuscript was laden with many dark themes and trauma, in particular mental and physical disabilities and illnesses and the complex emotions of a family coping with these challenges. I read the early drafts of the manuscript several times, taking notes as I read when images wafted up from the pages as I read.

In time, these led to pencil sketches, sometimes with the aid of historical research or by consulting Mas's family photographs. Relief printmaking requires that the image on the block be the reverse of my final desired image, so I usually scan the sketch, horizontally flip it, and then generate a LaserJet print at the desired size to fit the linoleum block. I tape the LaserJet print to the uncut block of linoleum then trace over the lines using a ballpoint pen and a sheet of old-fashioned carbon paper to transfer the drawing to the block. I often rework the transferred image with a pencil to refine lines and clarify negative and positive space before I sharpen my carving tools, made specifically for block carving. All of the negative spaces in the drawing will be carved away and print as "white" (the color of the paper I print on) and the remaining uncarved surfaces will print "black" (the color of the ink).

Once a clean image is on the block, I use a beveled, v-shaped gouge to cut along the edge of the lines of the drawing, occasionally switching to a very narrow gouge for the finest lines or even an angled blade to sometimes trace shapes. Finally, I use a wide, u-shaped scoop gouge to clear large areas of negative space. On average, the carving and printing of a single image requires about twelve hours of work, although I find the discipline meditative and deeply satisfying, requiring concentration and skill—one slip of the tool and a valuable piece of the raised linoleum carving could be lost forever.

After the block is cut and I've prepared my paper (for this project, I used Japanese *kozo* fiber paper handmade by Shotwell Paper Mill in San Francisco) and rolled out my ink (I used Van Sons rubber-based ink), I'm ready to print. Using an ink knife, I carefully take a modest amount of ink from the can and dab it onto the press's rotating ink drum, which is used to transfer ink onto the block in thin, even layers. *Kozo* paper is exquisitely thin and highly absorbent, so very little is needed to sufficiently ink up the lino. The press has built-in paper guides for ease of registration of the paper and the block and allows me to roll the press tympan with the paper attached over the block, resulting in a crisp linoleum block print.

There are 34 linoleum block prints in the final book, which I hope convey both the tenderness of touch and the resolute strength of a hundred-year-old grapevine, toughened by the seasons

The *Temples* illustration is directly inspired by a rare photograph from the Masumoto–Sugimoto family collection, depicting Jiichan Sugimoto's assortment of miniature wooden temples that once graced their gardens. It is probably the only extant image of Mas's grandfather's masterful carpentry skills, as the buildings did not survive the war, likely the victims of thieves. In the original photograph, Mas's aunt Hisako posed before the temples, but in this image, I have placed Shizuko and her brother Satoru playing.

I drew and carved the *Baachan in Gila* image immediately upon returning from my first visit to the remains of the Gila River Arizona concentration camp, where both Mas's and my family were incarcerated. War veteran memorial clean up, painting over graffiti, cleaning up broken glass and tossed soda cans, high on a hill in the desert. As members of the group looked down onto the former foundations of the barracks, mess halls, showers and toilets, and recreation halls, I quietly took a small sheaf of family photos from my backpack, black-and-white relics of my grandmother, step-grandfather, and my five-year-old father and his three-year-old brother. I lined up mountains in the photos with mountains on the actual horizon and counted saguaros.

Tankō Bushi is the name of a beloved folk dance that originated in Kyushu prefecture of Japan and is still performed by thousands of Japanese Americans every summer at the Buddhist *Obon* festival, which honors the spirit of one's ancestors. Although the dancer mimics the gestures of a coal miner digging, the lyrics are poetic and the story it tells is romantic. For this illustration, I wanted to show the *tankō bushi* being performed using real shovels (at *Obon* we "air dig" with our hands, using imaginary tools) against the backdrop of the Central Valley farmlands. My husband and five-year-old son, who have attended *Obon* many years counting, were my lovely models.

ACKNOWLEDGMENTS

David Mas Masumoto

This story and book would not have been possible without the help of family. First, my own family, Marcy my wife and our two children, Nikiko and Korio, all journeyed with me through these stories as we together explored a shared history and ancestry together. Also part of this tale includes the extended Masumoto family—we continue to be a farm family with memories embedded in these lands and a sense of place that can never be removed from our family legacy.

The Sugimoto family lies at the heart and soul of this book. From my grandparents to the many aunts, uncles and cousins—each family gathering contributed to this unfolding tale as we continue to define and redefine the meaning of family. My cousins, Gail Sakamoto and Lisa Sugimoto, shared some insight into family histories as did as my late sister, Shirley, who also provided observations and reflections from growing up in a very tightly close-knit family. Piecing together fragments of family stories instills a gratitude for all our perspectives, opinions, and secrets. A very special thanks to Uncle George Sugimoto and Aunt Lorrie (Lorada) Sugimoto Inouye who helped me work through this family saga. As Shizuko's siblings, they provided observations and opinions along with a keen sense of history that I will always cherish. And my mother, Carole Sugimoto Masumoto allowed me to keep asking questions and shared as many stories, emotions, and meanings as she could in an open and honest way. She passed away while I was writing this book, and I hope my words would bring a gentle smile of approval from her. Her soft hands joined my hands as each chapter unfolded.

The beautiful and detailed artwork of Patricia Wakida help to complete this book. Each print allows the story to grow and expand, the way a great partnership and collaboration works. She is part of this story—and her family including husband Sam and son Takumi Arbizo added their spirits to these illustrations.

I also want to acknowledge others who played a role in this book. Miriam Pawel, Jim Quay, Ken Hanada, Jenny Xu, Elizabeth Wales, Neal Swain, Mas Hamasu, Sue Dings, Ranee Johnson, and the Gila River Indian Community. A special thanks to Jose Andres, Julie Otsuka, Lawson Fusao Inada, and Amy Stolls.

Caregivers wonderfully shared stories with me and continue to provide much for others—Marla Markham, Tara Slocum, Mary Madden and Steve Sams. Without many other caregivers, Shizuko's life and story would have been lost.

I want to acknowledge the team at Red Hen who helped publish this story: Kate Gale, Mark E. Cull, Natasha McClellan, Rebeccah Sanhueza, Tobi Harper, Monica Fernandez, Tansica Sunkamaneevongse, Amanda De Vries, and Kamyar Jarahzadeh.

A special note of thanks to Alice Wong who helped to advance my thinking and perspectives about people with disabilities. I still have much to learn.

Also special thanks to family members who supported this work and publication—their contributions represent the joy and foundation for family ties that bind and are reinforced for generations to come. Warm hugs to: George Sugimoto, Lorada Sugimoto-Inouye, and the Sugimoto Family Trust; Lisa, Don, and Garrett Nose-Sugimoto; Nathan Sugimoto family—Nate, Chris, Lindsay, Alyssa, Jackson, and Aaron; Gail and Paul Sakamoto; Russell Sugimoto; Sandra and Joe Chambers; Mark and Ginny Sugimoto; Dennis and Jamie Sugimoto; Susan and Gordon Hayashi; Nancy and Jeff Kane; Teri and David Yasuda; Denise Masumoto and Toné Mosley; Judy and Joe Gehman, Linda and Paul Kimura, Leslie and Carlos Perez.

And in memory of Aunt Yoshi and Uncle Herky Yamagiwa.

And finally, I hope this story pays tribute to all our ancestors and a shared history of challenges. We strive not for just acceptance but to belong, much like Shizuko.

ACKNOWLEDGMENTS

Patricia Wakida

My warmest thanks to David Mas Masumoto, a true force of nature, for inviting me to collaborate, for our many conversations on family secrets and camp history, and most of all, for trusting in the maker to create a visual language to accompany Shizuko's story. To Yonsei Memory Project, for keeping me buoyant. Lawson Fusao Inada, thank you for bartering poems and memories of old Fresno families on a syncopated, jazz highwire. Thanks to my mom, Gerry, and dad, Don, for the care with which you raised the family in foggy Fresno, where we picked raisin stems in front of the TV all winter long. And to Sam and Takumi, infinite love.

I could not have completed this work without a special circle of family and friends who nurtured and supported this creative collaboration of art and words, by making it possible for me to create this series of linoblock prints and for supporting the publication of this book.

Deepest gratitude to: Mary Austin; Susan and Craig Bigham, in memory of Tamaye Kawakami (Okamura) and Yukio Kawakami; Hella Heart Oakland Giving Circle; Jeff and Debbi Jorgensen; Rod and Kathy Kebo; Larry and Janice Kebo; The Ito Roark Family, in memory of Kikuko and Masaji Ito; Lisa Sasaki, in honor of the Nitta and Fukuhara families; Wendy Tokuda, in honor of the Tokuda and Inouye families.

ABOUT THE AUTHOR

David Mas Masumoto is an organic farmer, author, and activist. His book *Epitaph for a Peach* won the Julia Child Cookbook award and was a finalist for a James Beard award. His writing has been awarded a Commonwealth Club of California silver medal and the Independent Publisher Books bronze medal. He has been honored by Rodale Institute as an "Organic Pioneer." He has served on the boards of the James Irvine Foundation, Public Policy Institute of California, Cal Humanities, and the National Council on the Arts with nomination by President Obama too. He farms with his wife Marcy and two adult children, Nikiko and Korio. They reside in a one-hundred-year-old farmhouse surrounded by their 80 acre organic peach, nectarine, apricot, and raisin farm outside of Fresno, California.

ABOUT THE ILLUSTRATOR

Linoleum block and letterpress artist Patricia Miye Wakida grew up in Fresno, California. In addition to maintaining her own linoleum block and letterpress studio under the wasabi press imprint, she frequently writes about Japanese American history and culture. She is a Yonsei (fourth-generation Japanese American), whose parents were incarcerated as children in the Jerome (Arkansas) and Gila River (Arizona) World War II Japanese American concentration camps. She lives in Oakland, California with her husband and son, cats, and chickens. Her website: www.wasabipress.com

Printed in the USA
CPSIA information can be obtained
at www.ICGtesting.com
JSHW021754130924
69717JS00005B/6

9 781636 281032